Scotland's Grand Slam 1990

Scotland's Grand Slam 1990

IAN McGEECHAN, DAVID SOLE AND GAVIN HASTINGS
with Ian Robertson and Mick Cleary

In association with

The Royal Bank of Scotland

STANLEY PAUL
London Sydney Auckland Johannesburg

Stanley Paul & Co. Ltd
An imprint of Random Century Group Ltd
20 Vauxhall Bridge Road, London SW1V 2SA

Random Century Australia (Pty) Ltd
20 Alfred Street, Milsons Point, Sydney 2061

Random Century New Zealand Limited
PO Box 40-086, Glenfield, Auckland 10

Century Hutchinson South Africa (Pty) Ltd
PO Box 337, Bergvlei 2012, South Africa

First published 1990

Set in Linotronic Ehrhardt by SX Composing Ltd, Rayleigh, Essex

Printed and bound in Great Britain by Butler & Tanner, Frome and London

British Library Cataloguing in Publication Data
Robertson, Ian 1945-
  Scotland's Grand Slam 1990.
  1. Scotland. Rugby union football
  I. Title II. Cleary, Mick
  796.33309411

ISBN 0 09 1746493

Contents

*The Princess Royal and her son Peter flanked by the SRU Secretary Bill Hogg (left)
and SRU President Jimmy McNeil before the Fiji match*

Foreword by HRH The Princess Royal

During the past two decades I have attended a variety of top sporting events, sometimes as a competitor or administrator though more often nowadays as a spectator; however I cannot recall an occasion which has evoked quite the same highly charged and emotional atmosphere as the Calcutta Cup match at Murrayfield on March 17th of this year. It seems the Scottish side that day were inspired not just by the huge partisan crowd but also by the good wishes and high expectations of the whole Scottish nation and Scots in every corner of the Commonwealth.

After all, this was the first time ever that two of the four Home Unions had reached their final game of the season with both of them capable of completing the Grand Slam. It seemed inevitable that the match would produce an unforgettable and historic contest and the game will live in everyone's memory for a very long time to come, hopefully for the right reasons.

For Scottish supporters, the victory against England was naturally the highlight of a wonderful season, but for me I have to say that I thoroughly enjoyed all three of the internationals which I watched in 1990. I can readily recall great tries and dramatic moments in the matches against France and Wales and these victories, along with the win in Dublin, were just as significant as the ultimate victory over England. This book is the tale of a fantastic season told by the man who coached the side, Ian McGeechan, and embellished with revealing comments from the captain David Sole and the vastly experienced full-back Gavin Hastings. It is the team's own account of what went on and, as such, gives an illuminating insight into all the events which surrounded this remarkable year.

Scotland may well collect a few more Grand Slams before the turn of the century to add to those of 1925, 1984 and 1990 but, just in case they don't, this book will serve as an admirable testament to remind everyone of the heroic deeds of the players who swept all before them in the space of six spectacular weeks. In warmly congratulating the players on their marvellous achievement, I look forward to sharing further success with them in the future.

Anne

Introduction

The Royal Bank of Scotland pioneered sponsorship of international Rugby as far back as 1902 when Scotland met Fiji, for the first time, at Murrayfield. Since then, there have been twenty-six Royal Bank Internationals in Edinburgh and eight seasons of the Five Nations Championship.

Those seasons brought two of the only three head-to-head confrontations in the whole of Rugby history and both were Royal Bank Internationals – Scotland against France in 1984 and against England in 1990.

No sponsor could ask for more, although we as a Group did go beyond the normal responsibilities of a sponsor and supplied, from among our employees, a player for each triumph – Keith Robertson in 1984 and Tony Stanger in 1990.

Not even the heady season of 1984 (and Scotland, remember, had not won a Grand Slam in the life-time of any of its players or indeed of some of their parents!) could compare with the dramatic scripting of 1990. The climax could not have been more tingling – the adversary not the Auld Ally as in 1984 but the Auld Enemy. Accordingly, St Patrick's Day 1990 was, inappropriately enough, the first ever occasion on which the prize for each side was to be Grand Slam, Triple Crown Championship and Calcutta Cup.

The story of that match and that season is one which Scots in particular will not tire of telling. This book splendidly recaptures the build up and climax of Scotland's finest international achievement. We at the Royal Bank of Scotland are proud to be associated with both the season and the book.

SIR MICHAEL HERRIES
Chairman
The Royal Bank of Scotland

1. The Build-Up

The final whistle at Murrayfield on 17 March 1990 was unquestionably one of the happiest moments of my rugby career, both as a player and as a coach, and, curiously enough, much of the basic groundwork for that historic and momentous occasion had been done with the British Lions in Australia the previous summer.

It was on that tour that I began to appreciate that there was very little wrong with British rugby that a few good wins in the Southern Hemisphere would not put right. My first task as the Lions' coach was to instill confidence into the team and a tour record of 11 wins out of 12 matches meant that by the end of thc trip, thc party talked eagerly and optimistically about their chances of victory should they be offered a crack at the All Blacks.

I honestly and genuinely believed that everything we had worked at for two months in Australia was just beginning to come together and click by the time of the last game against the Anzacs. I felt if we could have had another two or three weeks together we would definitely have been a match for the World Champions. More significantly, all the players in the party shared that belief. They believed in themselves and in British rugby, and were simply oozing confidence by the end of the tour.

You have to remember that this was the first Lions tour for six years so not since 1983 had the collective strengths of British rugby been tested in the international arena. Even the defeat in the First Test in Sydney played a role. It showed everyone that you can only

'If you do it this way, lads, you'll go through the whole season unbeaten,' suggests Ian McGeechan

make plans for one match at a time and it also showed how important it was to learn all the lessons from one game as you prepare for the next. We did that for the rest of the Lions tour, and then we did exactly the same for Scotland in the warm-up matches against Fiji and Romania and throughout the Five Nations Championship.

Confidence is crucial in international rugby and it was very re-assuring to me that the Lions were in buoyant mood when they assembled, two and a half months after the last game in Australia, to play France in a one-off match in Paris in October. When you con-sider that not a single member of the Lions squad that day had ever played in a winning side against France in Paris it speaks volumes for the new self-confidence of everyone that they went into that match fully expecting to win handsomely. This is precisely what they did.

I realized during the Lions tour that the great strength of British rugby in 1989 lay in Scotland and England. After all, they provided virtually two thirds of the whole Lions party and by the time we picked our strongest side for the Third and final Test there were 12 Scots and English in the team and three Welshmen.

I was delighted in October as we laid down our plans for the forth-coming season to know that I had an experienced core of nine battle-hardened Scots, six of whom had played in the Test series in Austra-lia, full of confidence and dedicated to the Championship, who had come through the Lions tour with flying colours. They had all emerged from Australia better players with a new sense of purpose and they were in the perfect position to help and inspire the rest of the Scottish squad as we began preparations for the Fiji game.

Furthermore, the Scots had benefited from sharing some of the Lions' problems. Scotland don't have four giant lineout men and we often rely on imagination, enterprise, variation and inspiration to claim our fair share of possession. Similarly, the Lions against Aus-tralia's row of skyscrapers – Cutler, Campbell, Gardner, Gourley, and Tuynman – had to introduce plenty of variety in our lineout play. By constantly shifting the target areas at the lineout, we kept the Australians guessing right through the final two Tests. We also shifted the target areas in the open to confuse the Wallabies further. In the First Test we would win a lineout and simply feed the scrum-half. In the Second Test, we regularly caught the ball and drove for-ward through the middle of the lineout to give the backs better pos-session. In the Third Test, the Wallabies anticipated this, so we changed the direction of our attack. We drove round the front and through the back with Dean Richards and David Sole the key men, as well as occasionally driving through the middle. We had different target areas for the scrums as well. Sometimes the scrum-half would break himself supported by the loose forwards, occasionally the number eight and flankers would lead the assault supported by the half-backs, sometimes the half-backs would unleash the three-

One of the five penalties Gavin Hastings kicked in the Lions Third Test win against Australia in 1989

quarter line and sometimes they would tactically kick or bring the ball back to the forwards. The key was to have plenty of variety, several alternative target areas and total discipline. This meant the Australians were never quite sure what we were going to do with our scrum or lineout possession and that put us firmly in control. This set-piece domination and the varied way in which we used it enabled us to win most of the second-phase possession. When you consider that the whole of our Grand Slam back row (Calder, White and Jeffrey) plus our half backs (Chalmers and Armstrong) were on the Lions tour, you can appreciate the benefit that the tour was for Scotland in the 1990 season.

Now, although these principles applied equally to Scotland as to the British Lions, I'm the first to admit the Scottish pack lacks the height, weight and sheer bulk of the 1989 Lions pack. So we knew we had to make up for our relative lack of size with superior individual and collective mobility in the open. That was critical in all our six victories from October onwards. It is also worth stressing that speed across the field and the fiercely competitive, combative edge was not just when going forward in attack but also in defence. I would hazard a guess that our tight five forwards pulled off as many tackles in the open as most of the other tight forwards from the other four countries in the Championship added together. These were the lessons the Scottish team learned from the Lions tour in Australia and they were fundamentally important as we began our pursuit of the Five Nations Championship in January; it is only fair to point out that talk of Grand Slams and Triple Crowns did not surface until March.

✿ The Royal Bank of Scotland
Fiji

In selecting the side to play Fiji we chose seven British Lions and the core of what I expected to be our side for the Five Nations Championship. As it turned out we made only one change for the Ireland game in Dublin in February – Finlay Calder returning to the side in place of Graham Marshall. I was pleased we had had the conviction the previous season to pick two new, young, inexperienced halfbacks, in Craig Chalmers and Gary Armstrong. They had a fantastic first season and thoroughly deserved their Lions tour at the end of it. But I was conscious that it is always very much harder to maintain that momentum the following season when the opposition will be preparing a special reception committee for such talented individuals.

I stressed how important it would be for both of them to do all the simple, straightforward things well and to establish their control, discipline and authority from the start of the Fiji game right through to the Calcutta Cup clash. Their decision making had to be very precise and their general tactical appreciation pretty tight. In the end it was, and from now on they can look forward to a long and glittering career together as a partnership because despite their age they now have loads of experience behind them, with plenty of Scottish caps, a Lions tour and the Scottish tour to New Zealand. Now they can switch from their natural instinctive attacking skills to a more disciplined approach whenever the occasion demands.

Chris Gray on the attack against Fiji with Damian Cronin in support

For the Fiji game I wanted the team to concentrate on control. There is no country in the world better at capitalizing on opposition mistakes and making something out of nothing than Fiji. Just as I had looked for forward control and discipline from the Lions in the Second and Third Tests against Australia, so I wanted Scotland to gain similar domination against the Fijians. This is not to say that I felt we would lose if it was an open, running, loose game; it is just, with one eye on the Five Nations Championship, I knew it was important for the team to learn to establish a solid platform up front and to be in a position always to dictate the pattern of play.

The Fijian match was a significant exercise for the team and I was very satisfied with the way things went. The onus on our forwards was to win quality possession in the set-piece play, which gave us the initiative in the loose play and left Fiji trying to play the game on the back foot most of the time on the retreat. For every match I have a list of priorities and top of the list against Fiji was control up front and once we had secured possession making certain we kept possession and the opposition never got the opportunity to win it back.

We determined to be as effective in attack as possible with loads of support play to keep the ball available, whilst when Fiji did win some set-piece ball making it as difficult and claustrophobic as possible for them to do anything with it. We wanted plenty of continuity and we worked hard at keeping possession, supporting the ball-carrier on both sides and after sucking in their loose forwards, creating space and freedom for the backs. The players gave a very positive response against Fiji and by sticking to our pre-determined tactics for the bulk of the game we put them under intense pressure, stretched them to the limit and ran in some very convincing tries.

Another priority for that match was our reaction to each piece of possession, whether it was ours or theirs. One great strength of our play had to be speed around the field throughout the match, our general pace and mobility and our speed of reaction to each and every situation was vital. I thought if we could match the Fijians for speed to the loose ball we would be in for a good performance.

I wanted the players to assert themselves in every contact situation just the way the All Blacks do, which means having collective support in both defensive and attacking situations. I emphasized the need to protect the ball when we were setting up second-phase possession and to make sure not only that we supported the man with the ball but also that he presented it to the next player accurately and at exactly the right moment. Instant decisions need to be taken to ensure continuity; and that continuity has been the key to our game and the hallmark of our success this season. Should the ball-carrier give a quick short pass, or should he let the ball be smuggled away by his colleagues in a close-quarter situation, or should he go to ground for a rapid ruck to let the backs spin the ball wide? It has all been about

Fijian lock Mesare Rasari outjumps Chris Gray at Murrayfield in October

Gavin Hastings scores against Fiji watched by his brother, Scott

instant decisions.

Again progressing from the experience on the Lions tour I believed that the presentation of the ball in the open was important. If we could produce greater pace and mobility in our pack and the ball was presented properly to the support players then we would discover the continuity I felt was essential if we were to win the Championship. We achieved all our priorities to a certain extent, and ran out good winners, restricting Fiji to two late tries in the last quarter of an hour of the match.

On the other hand, we ran in six tries with Tony Stanger scoring two and there was one each for Gavin Hastings, Iwan Tukalo, Kenny Milne and Chris Gray. I was also pleased that we had tactical control up until those final few minutes and we didn't kick away hard-earned possession to give Fiji the opportunity to counter-attack because that is exactly when the Fijians are at their most lethal. In retrospect, I set the team certain goals for the Fijian match and by and large we achieved them. We dictated the course of the game, we were always in control and in the driving seat and played the game the way we wanted to and in doing so we contained Fiji until their final flourish in the closing minutes, by which time we had built up a handsome lead.

✿ The Royal Bank of Scotland
Romania

Six weeks later at Murrayfield we faced a very different challenge from Romania and we had to adopt a different plan of campaign. Whereas Fiji revel in a loose, fluid match, Romania tend to concentrate on solid, tight set-piece play. Their strength is solid scrummaging, well-organized lineout possession and a barrage of varied tactical kicks from half-back to turn the opposition, drive them back and keep them on the retreat under pressure.

I decided that we were certainly good enough to match them in the set-pieces and it would be to our advantage thereafter to open the game up, run the ball wide, increase the tempo of play, concentrate on keeping the ball alive so there was plenty of continuity and make sure we dictated the pace of the game. I wanted to break up their pattern of set-piece kicking, chasing and forcing our players into errors. They would want to take the pace out of the game – I wanted Scotland to inject real, unrelenting pace into the game.

As with the Lions in Australia, it was necessary to introduce variety into our lines of attack and this meant there were occasions for the forwards to win lineout ball and feed Gary Armstrong in

stantly; other occasions to take and drive through the middle; and other occasions to peel round the front or the back. From scrums, the number eight, the flankers and the scrum-half had the range of different attacking options which meant Romania were never quite sure what we were going to do.

Gary Armstrong finds a gap with one of his cunning tactical kicks

With thoughts on the domestic Championship looming large by this stage I emphasized the need against Romania to have collective strength and speed in everything we did. It would be useless against England arriving slowly in dribs and drabs, in ones or twos, so now was the time to practise racing in numbers to the breakdown whether going forward in attack or back in defence. By that, I was looking for three or four players arriving together, followed almost instantly by the next couple. If we were perhaps not going to be bigger, stronger, or heavier than the English or even the French pack, it was vital we were yards faster to give us the initiative on every occasion in the loose.

We worked on this for the Romania match and tried to increase our mobility, backs and forwards, from that game in early December right through to the end of the season. Another priority against Romania was to build up an impregnable defence, initially with the

Derek White scores against Romania

*Doug Wylie halts the progress of Romania's Nicolae Fulina at Murrayfield
in December*

back row and half-backs in the set-pieces on the opposition ball and eventually through our back division as well. We talked at length about the first-tackle philosophy and the follow-up-tackle philosophy to put the opposition on the rack at every conceivable opportunity so they had no time to think or room to move. I have always been a great believer in sitting on the gain line and slotting in the tackles as quickly and emphatically as possible.

Against Romania we concentrated on this first-tackle responsibility and our commitment, organization and determination were such that in man-to-man marking and follow-up defence I reckon I can count all the missed tackles by Scotland in those six internationals of the 1989-90 season on the fingers of one hand.

The fact that we beat Romania 32–0 suggests our offensive defence was a success which was to stand us in good stead throughout the Championship. This was the first time the opposition had failed to score against Scotland since 1964 when both France and New Zealand were denied any points in internationals at Murrayfield. What is more, against stuffy defenders we scored five very good tries and with slightly better finishing we could have had one or two more.

Nevertheless, I was satisfied with the performance even if we did ease off a little near the end. I was also pleased that we had had two impressive wins over Fiji and Romania playing against totally different kinds of opponents, posing different sorts of problems, and we reacted with a quite different set of priorities for each game which helped to develop our adaptability and flexibility.

There is no doubt that these two internationals were a very good preparation for the home Championship, suitably complemented by the District Championship and the Trial at Murrayfield in early January. At this point we had one major decision to make and that was whether to return the captaincy to Finlay Calder who had been unavailable for the Fiji game or stick with David Sole who had done an excellent job in protecting and looking after the younger players whilst at the same time bringing out the best in the more experienced members of the side.

We opted for David Sole, partly because he had done so well as captain and was likely to be around until at least the 1991 World Cup, whereas Finlay had made it clear that this was to be his last season; and partly because without the captaincy Finlay could concentrate totally on recapturing his Lions form without the added responsibility of looking after the interests of the other 14 members of the Scottish side. I discussed it all with Finlay and he immediately threw his full support behind David, as did all the senior players. The team spirit, confidence and morale were really high, and we were one happy united family as our thoughts turned in mid January first to the Irish match in Dublin and then to the rest of the season.

Tony Stanger and Sean Lineen try to confuse the Irish in Dublin

2. Ireland v. Scotland

(Played for The Century Quaich Trophy donated by The Royal Bank of Scotland in 1989 to celebrate The 100th Match between the two Unions)

Scotland did not take the lead until ten minutes before the end when number eight Derek White scored his second try of the match. Even then Ireland almost drew level but Michael Kiernan missed a penalty goal just moments before the final whistle. It was a rather scrappy game all round. Ireland took the lead when Kiernan kicked a penalty in the seventh minute. Prop forward John Fitzgerald scored a try for Ireland just before half-time when he fell on a ball which had popped out of the side of a ruck on the Scottish line. Scotland came back in the second half. White scored after good work by Sean Lineen. Chalmers converted. Kiernan and White then exchanged penalties. White pushed the game Scotland's way when he shot off from the back of a scrummage to score in the corner.

I was worried about the Irish match. We were the last into the Championship, Ireland already had two quality games under their belt – New Zealand and England – and we were away from home. I had only won away from home once in all my playing days, so I was acutely aware of the problems. You're on an unfamiliar ground with an unfamiliar routine beforehand. During the match itself you can so easily get lured into the type of game the opposition want you to play rather than establishing your own preferred pattern. With the crowd against you it's very difficult to find the singlemindedness to establish control.

Sitting out the first round of the Five Nations is always a problem.

No matter how hard you make training, it can never match the pace and intensity of a Five Nations game itself. The whole tempo of the games is vastly different from an ordinary match. It's definitely a yard faster, the hits come harder and quicker and you're desperately struggling to exert some measure of control. We'd had two warm-up games ourselves against Fiji and Romania, but the opposition were not of the same calibre. Furthermore, they were played in half-empty stadiums which meant that there was little atmosphere or even pre-match hype. The Five Nations is a totally different experience.

The build-up for the game really began as soon as the trial finished a month earlier. Getting the correct XV is a key part of the whole process. We had deliberately put Finlay Calder and John Jeffrey into the junior side. I wanted to see them under a bit of pressure. It doesn't do them any harm at all to know that the young pretenders can perform a bit and are after their places. Finlay said to me that the trial really made him get things together. He and JJ (John Jeffrey) were on the back foot for the whole game and they suddenly realized what they were up against.

Selection is done by committee. We never have a vote, however. The other members of the selection committee will rarely go against what the coaches want. We argue and discuss and keep at it until we agree on the best XV. The back row obviously occupied a lot of our time. The senior back row in the Trial had played very well without Finlay and JJ but we felt that the experience the two Lions had had in the trial would sharpen rather than dull them. I suppose if we had just gone on the Trial showing we would not have selected them. But we figured that they were going to be far more motivated players for it. Of course their own massive experience was a major factor. We knew also that they were just getting back into things and were re-establishing their fitness. It was good to see that their appetite for the game had been renewed. Mentally they needed a break after the Lions tour and now here they were raring to go. That they both went on to have one of their best ever seasons shows just how much they applied themselves. The Trial really did create a healthy, competitive atmosphere.

Once we'd got the side sorted out everything focused on Ireland. I always take each game as it comes, planning for a particular opposition on a particular day with a particular set of players. How the other sides in the Championship are performing and what we might have to do when we eventually meet them does not interest me. You have to channel all your energies and thoughts into the next match.

Ireland would be tough. They were already heavily into the swing of things, had performed well for 65 minutes against England and I was not sure at what level we were capable of pitching it. I work very closely with the other coaches – Derrick Grant, Dougie Morgan and

Finlay Calder breaks clear against Ireland

Jim Telfer. The system works very well. I assisted Derrick Grant up to two years ago, before taking over the reins myself. Derrick wanted a break but we persuaded him to stay on the selection committee. You have to keep hold of the experienced men you have got, whether it be a player or a coach. Jim Telfer, who coached the Grand Slam side of 1984, came in with me last season to help with the forwards. Last January we had a long meeting to consider the next World Cup and things. Dougie Morgan agreed to help out with the three-quarters. I find the help invaluable. We bounce ideas off each other before I go away and plan the sessions. It's a very effective way of working.

We had a weekend at Gleneagles when the other countries were playing the first round of matches. It went well. We had invited Jim Blair to attend. Jim, who is a Scot, is fitness adviser to the All Blacks. He did a lot of work with the boys on the Saturday, after which we watched a recording of the England–Ireland match. We had intended to have just a brief chat for about 15 minutes afterwards asking Jim for his views on things. The whole thing just took off and

we were at it until after midnight. The players were fascinated by the New Zealand approach and attitude. They wanted to know how to become the best in the world and I'm sure that having Jim there helped to focus their minds on the battles ahead. Another thing that emerged from the discussion was in just how high regard Scotland are held in New Zealand. That view didn't do the boys' confidence any harm either.

You could sense that the players were beginning to get switched on to the Championship ahead of us. The Sunday morning session at Gleneagles went well with a lot of ball work. By now we were starting to put across ideas about the Irish match, things which we worked on again at Murrayfield a week later.

There were two key points to be made, I felt. One was that we had to work hard on our lineout play. The second was a much broader point, that we had to develop continuity.

Lineout possession is crucial. Unless you're desperately weak, scrum ball is predictable. The lineout ball is vital because if you don't get it, it is so hard to establish any sort of control on a game. You can't kick for touch, your moves are limited and your confidence takes a dive. Ireland were a good lineout side. Even England had struggled against them, and I knew from the Lions just how good Ackford and Dooley were. Ireland dropped Francis after the England game and brought in Lenihan. Donal, who had also been on the Lions tour, was a very experienced player so I knew there would be a problem there. Out of all the sides we played I would say that Ireland were one of the most effective in the lineouts.

Continuity was to be a key objective for us. We're not the best stop-start team. To be continually stopping for set-piece play did not suit us. Our aim was to keep the ball on the move using the back row and the midfield. To effect this the skill level had to be high throughout the side. To keep the ball on the move means that all the players have to concentrate very hard and be aware that they must be able to switch from ball handler to ball winner in a split second. I think our play during the season bore this out. At vital times, such as Damian Cronin's try against Wales, the forwards were able to handle the ball under pressure just like threequarters. And our first try against Ireland, scored by Derek White, came at the end of a 56-second sequence of play. I impressed on the players the need for 20-second bursts. That's a long time, in fact, and requires great mental and physical application.

The Sunday session at Murrayfield in the week before the Irish match was taken by Jim. It began like all the others with skill work. It's vital that players are used to having the ball in their hands. Players are split into groups of three or four, in small grids perhaps and I get them to pass, react quickly to instructions and maybe criss-cross on each other, passing. It's intensive stuff, the aim being to get them used to the pressures of a game where a ball comes to you from unexpected angles. I've always believed that the number on your back is irrelevant. It's the position you are in in relation to the ball which is crucial. If you're first there, then you become a wing forward, no matter what the number on your back might say.

I was a bit concerned before the Sunday session for various reasons. I was worried that the half backs – Gary Armstrong and Craig Chalmers – might not be quite sharp enough. Both had been injured and although they were fully fit again they had not had an awful lot of match practice.

My other concern that morning was personal. I was confined to bed and I felt dreadful. I'd been under the weather for a week or so and it soon became apparent that I would not make it to Dublin. The flu had hit. I was obviously disappointed not to be going to Dublin but I was happy that Jim Telfer would look after things properly, a man who has had such a massive influence on the development of players and coaches in the last decade.

That Sunday session was about two and a half hours long. It was longer than usual because, as always at the start of a campaign, there were a few things to talk through. As the season goes on everything tends to become more effective, so the sessions get shorter. Our last practice on the Friday before the Grand Slam match lasted only 35 minutes. I've never believed in staying out there just for the sake of filling up time.

It's always a bit strange before a Five Nations season starts. You are training in a vacuum in a way, just hoping that you've got it right. I talk to the players a lot because I need their feedback: first because they give me more ideas, and second to check that they understand what I'm trying to do. Jim Telfer will do a lot of work with the forwards, while I deal with the backs. But Jim and I will have spent hours on the phone making sure that both he and I are on the same wavelength. We generally are.

Scotland were booked into the Fitzpatrick Hotel at Dun Laoghaire. It's important that you find a hotel and training ground that you're happy with. Bob Munro, the chairman of selectors, had come over separately to check it out. It was the right side of Dublin in that we wouldn't have to cross the city to get to Lansdowne Road, it was not far from Blackrock College where we were to train on the Friday, and the facilities themselves were fine. I had made a point of checking out the menus beforehand. I ask the hotels to cut down on the carbohydrates, and also remind them to cut down on the portions. What tended to happen was that in their flush of hospitality they would overfeed us. This is one of the drawbacks about playing away from home, not really knowing the hotel and the set-up. Little things can unsettle players. I try to ensure that everything is in the best possible order. The players themselves are beginning to tune in to the

importance of diet throughout the year as well as in the 48 hours before a game. We never put any restrictions on alcohol. That's up to the players. In fact, the forwards will often go to the corner of the bar for a quiet drink and chat on the Thursday or Friday evening.

I believe the flight over was a bit hairy as the plane had to turn back to Edinburgh shortly after take-off. However, once there, things went well. Jim had a fairly steady session at Blackrock on the Friday. It's a smashing place to train because they make such a special effort to look after you. They make us feel really welcome, laying on tea and sandwiches for us. Everything was taken nice and gently on Friday, just getting the players organized and settled. A lot of time was spent on the set-pieces, making sure that everything was comfortable. Simple things like kick-offs and drop-outs were practised. I say simple but they are such a vital area. If you get them right then you end up 30 or 40 yards down the pitch rather than struggling on your own 22.

Meanwhile back home in Leeds I was feeling pretty edgy. I could have travelled to Dublin on the Saturday as I had shaken off the worst of the flu. I decided not to, however. I was worried that if I came in at the last minute I might disturb the players' routine too much. As you get nearer to a match it's important that the players themselves take over, get used to making decisions for themselves. It was better that I stayed put.

Watching the match on television was always going to be difficult. It was even more so as I had to sit through England–France first. When they switched to Lansdowne Road at the end, we just got highlights of the first half. John Fitzgerald scored a messy try for Ireland from the side of a ruck. It looked from our point of view a messy sort of game. We had no control at all in the lineouts so there was no chance to get hold of the game. There were some good things happening but only in fits and starts. It was all very frustrating. I am a terrible spectator at the best of times. This was the worst of all.

One thing would go right and then suddenly we'd make a mistake and be back to square one. Craig Chalmers was not having the best of times at fly half. It seemed that my concern about his lack of match sharpness was being borne out. You have to find your game very quickly at international level and I think Craig himself would admit that he never really got it together against Ireland. Since he has come into the side his kicking has been enormously important to us. In that first half though he was either 10 yards too short or 15 yards to the wrong side. The second season of international rugby is always the most difficult for a player. Craig and Gary had been a revelation the year before. Now teams were actually planning for them, so the two of them had to adapt accordingly. In a way Ireland taught us a bit here about the need to vary the game, not just to get one idea in our heads and stick with it.

Derek White crashes over the line for one of his two match-winning tries against Ireland

Ireland were giving us problems and we were giving ourselves problems by making errors. We were having problems with our goal-kicking as well. The decision to switch to Craig after Gavin Hastings had missed three times was the right one. We'd talked about the possibility beforehand. Craig was kicking very well for Melrose and his percentage success rate on the shorter kicks was very high. One of the mistakes we made though, which we recognized afterwards, was that we had to keep Gavin involved in the game. With Craig doing the place kicking as well as the touch kicking, it meant that Gavin didn't get involved in the game for a long

Irish full-back Kenny Murphy safely catches a towering up-and-under with Scott Hastings in attendance

time. We made sure that Gavin would do the line kicking thereafter. I thought Fitzgerald's try just before half-time which made the score 7–0 would make things really difficult for us. Ireland were all fired up, determined to show their supporters that they were better than their England performance.

At half-time we looked to be up against it a little. Crucially we changed our game plan in the second half. One of the reasons for our success last season was our ability to make decisions on the field. That's the great benefit of having some experienced players in there like Finlay and JJ. Whoever took the decision at half-time, be it the back row or David Sole, it was certainly the right one. They started to take the game to Ireland through the back row. We attacked them, knocked them backwards and suddenly we had found that extra yard. The pace stepped up and we found that vital continuity. Sean Lineen began to assert himself a bit more at inside centre. Being able to alter tactics when you're under pressure away from home is the hallmark of a very good side. Using the back row more was absolutely the right thing to do. As I said earlier, the play leading up to our first try lasted 56 seconds which is an excellent sequence of sustained play. I have spent a lot of time talking to the players about body clocks, about trying to operate in bursts of 20 seconds. That's often how we work it in practice. You get through a lot in 20 seconds. You cover a lot of ground, are maybe involved in four or five contact situations, use a lot of different skills and are constantly linking with other players. If the players manage to achieve such a passage of play in a match, then they feel as if they are in a game that is going their way. It's this business of feeling that things are right. Confidence is a vital factor in international rugby. It just wasn't there against Ireland in the first half. It was all stop-start with play being dictated by Ireland. Once we upped the pace we began to find more control.

The second try by Derek White was also very pleasing to see, quite apart from the fact that it put us in front. I reckon that Derek is the fastest number eight off the base, so if we could operate a good fast channel one ball from a scrummage, then we could be in business. So it proved against Ireland with Derek shooting past the Irish defence for his second try.

The ball that Derek takes is incredibly fast. It doesn't touch anyone's feet. It's literally a rolling ball off the hooker's foot with a pick-up on the move from Derek. It does mean that the other forwards have to be spot on in keeping the scrum tight and in position. If they move an inch then the move is in trouble. They were tremendous in holding tight.

Derek is a terrific footballer. It takes great skill to pick up a moving ball like that. Derek has probably had his best season ever in 1990. It was only his second full season at number eight . Having a regular slot at number eight had done his confidence no end of good.

Before, he was moved around from second row to flanker and so on. Being taken on the Lions tour as an out and out number eight meant a lot to him, to be recognized as an outstanding number eight in his own right.

The form of the back row all season has been crucial. We were seeing the first signs of their importance in the Irish match. Finlay worked very hard throughout and played a much tighter game all round. So too did John Jeffrey. JJ always liked a free-flowing loose game. One of his weaknesses was the tight stuff. This year some of the close-quarter work he did was crucial to our success. Without doubt I think it was his best season. Their form was also a tribute to Jim Telfer. Jim does a lot of work on body positions, how best to hit a ruck and maul. The forwards, particularly the back row, benefited enormously. They are very aware of the special interest Jim takes in their performances.

Those last few moments of the Irish match were pretty nerve-racking, particularly when Michael Kiernan missed a penalty just before the end. We held on and by the end I thought we'd come to terms not only with Ireland, but also with being back in the international arena again.

Jim Telfer said that the dressing room was like a morgue after the game. It was as if we had lost. Jim had to remind them they had just achieved Scotland's first away win for four years. It was good though that the players were so self-critical. If they have such pride in their own performance then it means that you are on the right path. The coaching job becomes so much easier.

As a coach at this level you're trying to put a picture of the way a game might develop into the players' minds. They then have to make decisions themselves on the field to bring about that picture. Against Ireland they felt that they had not really brought that together. Jim responded to their dejection magnificently. He sensed that they needed to get if off their chest straight away. So when they got back to the hotel after the match, he got them together for ten minutes to clear the air. Where do we go now? What must we do?

It was just the right thing to do. We adopted it for all the other games. Dump the luggage in the foyer, find a room straight away and just get stuck into it. A quick, gut reaction to what had just happened. It helped the players, and it helped Jim and me, to store away their very honest appraisals and set about planning the next session.

The lineout was an area of big disappointment. It wasn't the jumpers' fault but the players around them. They all felt that they had tended to operate in isolation, rather than getting in and around the jumper. They felt they'd been out-thought and out-fought a bit. We often got the first touch but hadn't responded positively enough. Jim and Derrick Grant analysed the video to see what was happening in the lineout off the ball, to see how players were reacting. As a

result of that game, Jim devised several drills to practise bringing all the forwards into the lineout more. When we wrote down priorities for the French match, the lineout was at the head of the list. We had to think and act as one.

Defensively, Ireland hadn't been a bad game for us. We showed that we could absorb pressure. The backs said that they never felt under real threat from Ireland in that department, that their defensive organization was up to anything Ireland had put their way. The backs use two or three different systems, depending on the opposition. Gavin Hastings took a crucial high ball late in that game which was important not just for the outcome of that match, but also

Finlay Calder leads this Scottish assault against Ireland with Paul Burnell and Chris Gray close at hand

to show that once again we had a firm foundation. It lends the rest of the side a lot of confidence if they know that things are secure at the back.

We didn't perform that well in attack in the sense that there was not the consistency to it. It improved in the second half but there was work to be done there. I was reasonably happy with the fitness of the players. They were not as sharp in the early stages but that was as expected. It takes some time to adjust to the increased pace of a Five Nations match. The players felt that they had a fair bit of running left in them in the last quarter of an hour.

The scrummage stood up well as the second try illustrated. Two of the unsung heroes all season were Paul Burnell at prop and Chris Gray in the second row. When you look at the games carefully and see all the extra little bits you get from both of them, then you realize their worth. The number of times that one, or both of them, would pop up when a ball was spilled in a tackle, or be the first to a player who had got himself isolated, was marvellous. Sean Lineen and Scott Hastings came together quite well in the match. I was a bit worried about Sean's form because he had not had a great District Championship for Edinburgh. Against Ireland he was so positive at inside centre, particularly the angle he ran at to create the opening for Derek White's first try. Sean also ran well off the back row.

It was all very strange for me to watch it from afar but I was reasonably happy because I knew from personal experience just how difficult it was to win away from home. Jim rang me almost straight after the game and told me how gloomy the players were. I think they were having to come to terms with the fact that they'd gone into the Championship as one of the favourites, which is something of a new experience. They were obviously responding to it in the right way. The worst thing possible would have been if they had got too many grand ideas about themselves and their abilities. Their attitude was obviously good.

The victory proved at least that the system was working. The players had altered the pattern of the match by themselves. That proved that we were not too dogmatic in our coaching. As a coach I'm just a servant to the players. My job is to make them as prepared as possible for a game in the way that they think, the tactics open to them and how they can adapt and make decisions.

One of the reasons we have been successful is that the players have always recognized the value of hard work. We have much smaller playing resources than some other countries. The players never lost sight of the need to prepare thoroughly and never to get too carried away by any success.

INTERVIEW WITH DAVID SOLE

ROBERTSON: *Scotland went into this match as hot favourites but in the end struggled to win. What do you think went wrong?*

SOLE: The whole team knew that we failed to hit peak form for the whole 80 minutes and we were particularly below par in the first half, but the most significant fact is we should not have been made hot favourites. I had played over 20 internationals for Scotland at the time but had never played in an away win in the Championship and in the past five years we had had only one away victory. Ireland were battle-hardened after tough matches against New Zealand in November and England in January, whereas we had played less arduous games against Fiji and Romania. We had also sat out the opening round of double internationals in January which meant we came into the Irish game cold and caught them on the rebound with a point to prove after their Twickenham defeat and they were in front of their own supporters. It took us most of the first half to adjust to the much faster pace and far tougher physical confrontation of a Five Nations Championship game.

ROBERTSON: *What would you say was the worst aspect of the Scottish performance?*

SOLE: There were two major disappointments. Firstly, I would say the general feeling in the side was that our lineout play was the most worrying part of our performance. We were outplayed in this area and it forced us to radically re-think our strategy for the remaining matches and I have no doubt our consequent dramatic improvement at the lineout in the next three games played a significant part in our ultimate success. Secondly, the other disaster area was our failure to take our chances which is so often the difference between winning and losing at international level. In the first half we pushed a couple of penalty kicks wide and we wasted a couple of great try-scoring opportunities in the top left-hand corner which I am sure later in the Championship we would have converted into points.

ROBERTSON: *What did you say at half-time when you were trailing 7–0 and defeat was a distinct possibility? Was there an element of panic or were you still confident?*

SOLE: Obviously we were a bit worried and I told the forwards to tighten their play, drive much more at the Irish and we needed to concentrate more on the strength of our back row. I believe it was the way the three loose forwards – John Jeffrey, Derek White and Finlay Calder – asserted themselves in the second half which helped to turn the tide. It certainly helped to produce the two match-winning tries for Derek White. We also knew at half-time we had to increase our speed around the field and bring our fitness into play.

ROBERTSON: *What did you feel at the final whistle?*

SOLE: An immense sense of relief that we had managed to win and after the initial feeling of despondency in the changing-room, a certain measure of optimism because everyone knew we could have and should have done far better than we did and we were capable of a great deal of improvement. It augured well for the future, just the fact that we had secured a rare away win whilst playing well below our best.

INTERVIEW WITH GAVIN HASTINGS

ROBERTSON: *Did you feel that it was a desperately close game because Ireland played well or Scotland played badly?*

HASTINGS: If you had seen our changing-room after the match you would have seen at once that although we were delighted to have won we were very disappointed with our overall performance. We definitely looked a shade rusty and the fact that we had had much easier warm-up games than Ireland and we had not played for two months prior to Dublin meant that we were not at our best. Without any disrespect to Ireland I think by the time we played England six weeks later we were a much better side and it was encouraging for us to win considering we did not play well. It's also fair to pay credit to Ireland because they played some very good rugby, especially at the lineout, which restricted our attacking options and they also tackled well to make life hard for us. They're always an incredibly difficult side to beat at home and having given the New Zealand All Blacks a run for their money in November it would be an insult to the Irish to suggest they were no-hopers before the game. The only possible criticism that could be levelled at the Irish is that they faded late on against New Zealand, England and us and I think our fitness gave us a significant advantage.

ROBERTSON: *Were you happy with the contribution by the Scottish backs?*

HASTINGS: I suppose with hindsight it was not one of our more inspirational efforts but our defence was excellent and you have to remember the conditions were difficult for running rugby. Firstly, we had problems at the lineout; secondly, there was a strong, unsettling wind to contend with; and thirdly, we were up against a very determined, very committed Irish side. In those circumstances, to have taken too many risks in attack which might have allowed the Irish to counter-attack in their best traditions could have been to their advantage.

ROBERTSON: *At what stage of the match were you confident of winning?*

HASTINGS: About five minutes after the final whistle. The Irish are fantastic competitors and never give up and even when we took the lead for the first time late on we never relaxed. My place kicking hadn't been all that clever and I remember my moment of truth came near the end when I had to catch a huge up-and-under and as I caught it with the Irish almost on top of me I could feel the whole Scottish pack arrive to support me and save the situation. Thanks to our level of fitness, determination and organization we were able to survive. And with this victory we had plenty to build on for the rest of the season.

Here Derek White scores his other try against Ireland

3. ✿ The Royal Bank of Scotland
Scotland v. France

Scotland took some time to get into their stride. They were only leading by a lone penalty goal when the French flanker, Alain Carminati, was sent off nine minutes into the second half for stamping on John Jeffrey's head. France had made ten changes after the heavy defeat by England. Scotland were unchanged. Gavin Hastings opened the scoring with a penalty goal from 45 metres in the tenth minute. Scotland had the advantage of a fierce wind in the first half but could not add to their score. Only a brilliant tap tackle by Chalmers on Hontas prevented France from scoring in the first half. With Carminati off the field, Scotland were able to stretch France. Calder scored a try after a kick ahead by Tukalo. Chalmers converted to add to the penalty he had scored following the Carminati incident. Tukalo himself scored after squeezing out of two tackles. Chalmers' conversion and second penalty goal ten minutes from time completed the scoring.

The week after an international is a very busy week. That is the time I do most of my planning. I'll sit down each night after the children are in bed and reach for the video. It's a great asset to have a video. It means that I can get to know the opposition inside out. With the remote control at the ready, I switch back and forth until I'm satisfied that I've understood a particular passage of play. I tend to analyse a video from a certain perspective. I'll maybe look at defensive patterns or line play or perhaps back-row work. It takes a good nine or

Craig Chalmers cuts through against France

ten hours to assess fully all the necessary video material.

For France I studied two videos carefully: their defeat by England of course, but also their victory in Cardiff. Teams, particularly the French, tend to play differently away from home so it's important to build that into your calculations. A lot of my notes are very rough at the beginning although I do have a shorthand system for the video. As the week progresses though, I tend to draw all these notes together in order to make a list of priorities for the Sunday training session. I also have a rough board in the kitchen so if something suddenly strikes me then I can jot it down quickly.

I'd had a long phone conversation with Jim Telfer on the Sunday after the Irish match. Normally the coaches would get together after the dinner on a Saturday evening for a chat about the week ahead. Then it's over to me and the video.

I set about watching France and England closely, but only from the French point of view. Once again it was not England who interested me at this stage in terms of what they were capable of doing. The match was illuminating because, although England had won handsomely, France had put England under pressure at various points. Interestingly, the English scrum was under pressure in the early stages. That meant that we had to be absolutely on top of our

scrummage game if we were to compete. Both sides in that match were working under pressure which is a key area to study. That's when you really see how they make decisions.

What made the analysis a little bit difficult was that France had not named their side and in fact didn't do so until after our Sunday session. Berbizier was dropped which was a critical factor. Camberabero came back in even though he had been dropped after the Welsh game. I thought he was unlucky to be left out. Mesnel was back in the centre which means that you've got two good thinking players in midfield with Sella working outside them. It was a far better midfield than the one which played against England.

It was the forwards who occupied a lot of my close study, however. France had played the two biggest packs in the Championship and pressurized them. They were basing a lot of their game around their forwards. They were playing close to the set pieces throughout the game, doing nothing wide at all. Everything they did was based around Berbizier. However, they were not playing that game particularly well. The first man through was often going to ground and getting isolated. That was what we had to work on then. Get them to ground quickly and isolate them.

The lineout was a targeted area. We'd been very hit and miss against Ireland which we were all determined to improve. More specifically, I wanted to counter the French system of driving round the back. I thought that if we put David Sole at scrum half on their throw

RIGHT: Serge Blanco won't hear of Sean Lineen beating him to the ball

Gary Armstrong attracts the attention of six French defenders

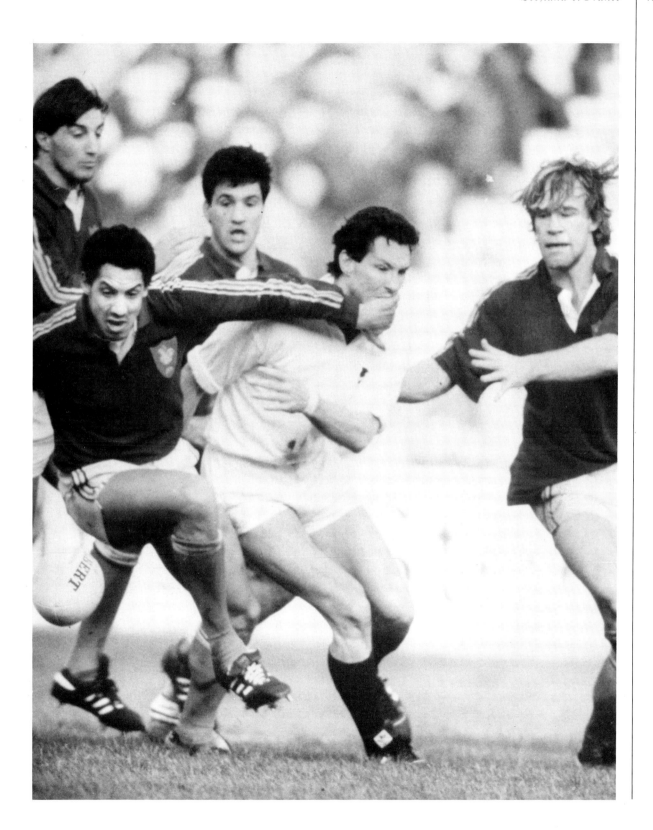

to sweep into the space at number six, put Kenny Milne into the lineout and move Gary Armstrong to the hooker's position, then we could block them. Finlay was at the back and had to counter their jump or knock them down as they came round. If not, then David was there. If, in fact, we stole their ball, then David Sole is a good passer anyway. It was a ploy designed to attack the French at one of their strong areas. We were going to pressurize their space. If it worked, it would upset them.

The lineout was also critical for another reason. Their forwards were slow. We had to work on speeding up the game which we hadn't achieved terribly well against Ireland. I felt we were taking too long to organize some of our lineouts. I devised a block of three or four lineouts which would be preordained. Once that sequence was set in motion there would be no call. Kenny would get his hands on the ball and throw. Everyone had to be on their toes. That would lift the pace of proceedings and keep their forwards on the move which they wouldn't enjoy.

The lineout was also important for another reason. I like to keep our own players on their toes, particularly at training sessions. If I can come up with something new it has a positive effect on them. They want things to be different; they enjoy talking and thinking new things through. Of course if it starts to come off in the match itself, it again lifts their confidence as they believe that the game is going their way.

We had been the most successful of the sides against France at home. They had not won at Murrayfield since 1978. That was a big advantage for us. It had arisen because we had always set out to play them in a particular way. You have to be clinical against France, re-mind yourself how good they can be on the attack, and then set out to attack them at their Achilles heel. Of course another coach may do it all differently. People do not have the same view on a match. All I'm worried about is that I can put my hand on my heart afterwards and say that Scotland were prepared to the best of my ability: that the players knew as much about the opposition as they needed and that they had a firm grasp of possible tactics. If they have all this in-formation, it lends a shape and purpose to their training.

I also spent a night in Edinburgh in the week after a match, for selection. I drive up from Leeds on a Tuesday afternoon and back down the following morning. It takes about four hours each way. Selection for the French game wasn't that difficult because I could see where we were going and the fifteen players from the Irish match were, at that point, the ones best able to carry that through. It hadn't come off against Ireland but I could see why. It was simply a question of sorting a few things out. The personnel were fine. It was just up to Jim and myself to change the emphasis a little.

I knew also from the players' reaction to the Irish game that they

John Jeffrey breaks through the first line of French defence and finds Derek White ready to carry on the good work

were hell-bent on getting things right. By the time we got to the Sunday session at Murrayfield, I knew what I wanted to see. I'd written down a list of priorities which I spent about 15 minutes or so putting across to the players. They are good listeners although, as ever, I'm always ready for feedback. They knew themselves the dangers of the French. They knew that we had to stop them getting any momentum. If they get into a rhythm then it just goes on increasing. You find forwards who have been lolling about the field suddenly spark into life. They are so aware of when something is on, more so than any other country. You get French props who know that if they get there, then they are in business. However if you block that momentum, then those players might disappear.

When things are not going well for France they can panic. It had happened against England. Berbizier set off 10 yards from his own

In a rare French break Laurent Rodriguez finds Kenny Milne in his way

line and got horribly tangled up. We knew that if we could tighten our own game and not make mistakes that might put the pressure on France a bit. Serge Blanco was obviously one player we focused on. He had always played well against us. He's very dangerous if he can run into the line. We had to sharpen up our kicking which had been a bit wayward against Ireland. We did not want to give him any space. We needed to put him under pressure so that when he did collect kicks he only had one option which was to kick for touch. I figured that if we could get the ball into an area 15–20 yards in from touch then we might cause problems. Blanco tends to stay in the middle of the field and the wingers stay wide. If we could hit that space between them then it might cause a bit of indecision. So whether it was Craig Chalmers, Gary Armstrong, or even Scott or Gavin Hastings, they had to hit the target. Either that or push him right back. If you can see the number on his shirt then it means that you are not doing too badly. As it turned out, it worked well. Blanco did not have a good game.

The Sunday training session is always a live one. By that I mean that there will be a lot of contact work done, using many players on the fringe of selection as the opposition. I've also made a point of inviting some of the under-21 players to attend that session to get them used to the senior set-up. Tony Stanger had come through that way the season before. Graham Shiel, a centre, Doddie Weir, Shade Munro and Andy McDonald in the second row have all had some very useful experience this season.

It's important that any side is put under pressure in training. They must be able to handle under intense pressure in a match and the only way to ensure that is by live practice. Of course, when you re-gather on a Wednesday evening you will only have the squad of twenty-one with which to work. You can get a lot of use though out of using contact bags. That Wednesday we worked with the forwards and the half backs at Murrayfield, doing a lot of set-piece work.

It takes two Frenchmen to slow down John Jeffrey as the Scots take control

We stay at the Braid Hills Hotel in Edinburgh which the players are very happy with. It's small and comfortable and the staff are re-

ceptive to the players. On Thursday we have a full session. I run over the list of aims and objectives again, stressing the need for an error-free performance. Continuity is again a major focus of attention. That Friday session we ran through kick-offs and drop-outs again. I also took the back rows away from the forwards for 20 minutes and got them working with the backs. The idea was to practise the links between them. Basically, I wanted to sharpen up their ball winning, to get them used to the idea that the nearest man, be it a back or whoever, would go in and rip the ball out. It was vital that we got an immediate reaction from whoever was nearest. The priority was speed and control on contact. We could not afford to lose a ball that we had won from a set piece or wherever. We knew the French would lap that up.

On Thursday evenings I go through videos with the players. I won't show them a whole match because it would take too long. It is much better just to highlight one or two features from a couple of games. I showed bits from our win in Ireland as well as passages from the two French games. It takes about an hour in all and I encourage comment from the players. Sometimes one of the players will actually trigger a conversation about how the play might develop from that situation. It certainly focuses the mind and reinforces a lot of what we had run through that day. On the Friday evening I'll

again have a short video session but this time only looking at our game, not the opposition's.

That Friday I also brought a board in to sketch out a few possible game situations. I then invited comment which fired off a couple of the other players as well. It's useful in that the forwards can see how the backs are thinking, and vice versa. They need to know the others' expectations and needs. My input on a Friday evening is finished by about six o'clock. You have to leave the players time to relax and for things to sink in. They often have a drink among themselves before dinner, before heading off into Edinburgh to the cinema.

Saturday dawned very windy. That disturbed me. Not because I thought we weren't capable of coping with it. Rather it's always much better to have a game of equal halves, a full 80-minute game. Once you've got severe wind you're looking at a 40-minute game and then adapting to the elements accordingly. That Saturday morning we talked about how we might play the game in those conditions. It's important at this stage that most of the talking is done by the players. They have to take over. And they did. They wanted to keep the French forwards on the move so the wind could help them there. Also with the ball hanging up in the wind it meant Blanco would have to stand about and wait for it to fall. Of course, they also considered how they would be on the rack once they turned into the wind.

We decided it would be best to have first use of the wind if we won the toss. This might not always be the best thing to do. It just depends on your objectives. We wanted to put some pressure on early so it suited us to win it and have the wind at our backs.

I was pleased with the way the first half went. That may sound surprising given that we turned round only 3–0 up. However, we had created chances. I suppose it was a bit of a worry that in the end we didn't get tries and that we missed a few kicks at goal. France had come close to scoring as well. They'd broken out well two or three times and if it hadn't been for that superb tackle by Craig on Hontas they would have been in front. It was a terrific tackle and showed how great our commitment is in defence. It's always the way with France – that one moment you're pressing in attack and the next moment you're in the depths of defence. That's why you always have to be so alert. At 3–0 at half-time we knew we had a game on our hands.

The crucial moment came just after the kick-off for the restart. No, not the Carminati incident. Before that. The big psychological turning point was Gavin's first kick. Blanco had been trying to kick France out of their 22 for the whole of the first half without much success. Then here was Gavin fielding the ball between the posts and thumping it down to the half-way line right up into the West Stand. You could see the look of disbelief on their faces. Cambera-

Half-time in the French game with Scotland leading only 3-0, and not a lot to shout about as they prepare to face the wind

bero just stared at it not believing that it could be possible. He was thinking, 'Hey, perhaps we're not going to spend all the second half in their 22.' In an instant they realized that they were going to have to reappraise how they were going to play the game. We followed that up by winning the lineout and driving at them. We actually spent six or seven minutes in and around half-way or else driving them back to their 22. That was something they'd not managed in the whole of the first half. The times they'd attacked had tended to be long, sweeping moves up the field before we knocked them back again.

Perhaps it was the frustration at not being in control when they should have been which sparked Carminati off. Those opening minutes of the second half had not gone the way they had expected. Also we were not making any mistakes so France had very little to work on. They were still playing the Berbizier type of game close to their forwards which we dealt with very well. We rarely, if ever, missed a first tackle. Having Sanz in there at scrum half didn't seem to have altered their strategy. They ignored Mesnel and Sella out in the centre.

A lot of people have commented that France lost the game rather than we won it. I disagree. As soon as Carminati went off, they looked as if they had 14 men. That's not always the case. Wales certainly hadn't looked that way when Moseley had been sent off against France. I think it was a big compliment to the team that we made it look obvious that France were a man short. I was worried that it might fire France up. It didn't because we didn't give them the opportunity. Our back row kept them on the turn, getting in behind them where the lack of a wing forward began to tell. We speeded up delivery again, generating some very quick ruck ball and really started to run at them. Our interlinking, which we'd worked on the day before, began to show through. It all paid off and we scored two tries.

We had physically stretched them and they were bound to crack. Once the scores came that was it because we retained control. The players themselves were much happier with their performance. They felt that they had imposed themselves on the game. It was interesting that the French journalists were complimentary about our play. They recognized that we had beaten France well which is always a good benchmark to have. I think that even if Carminati had stayed on we would still have won, although perhaps not by such a large margin. Maybe 9 or 12 to nil.

We repeated the 10-minute meeting the players had had after the Irish game. This time it was much more positive. They felt that even though they had been under some pressure in the game, they always had that measure of control. The fitness was good. When I studied the videos later I noticed that there were several occasions when a

Scott Hastings tries to burst through a French tackle with Finlay Calder at his elbow

French player was under extreme pressure because he was surrounded by five or six Scottish shirts.

The lineout went well. I think we won the first five on the trot. It's especially pleasing when an area you've targeted comes off. It's good for the players as well because it makes them feel that other areas might pay off as well. The forwards worked much more as a unit in the lineouts. The jumpers were able to jump where they wanted to. Against Ireland they'd had their space taken away from them.

We hadn't really got as wide as we would have liked in either game. The wind had obviously had a bearing on that but even so there was work to do there. Craig and Gary were much more attuned at half back. We were playing a very different way from last year which was as much to do with the fact that the opposition were taking us more seriously. They saw us as a real threat this year and they worked much harder on closing us down.

All round, everything was on a sound footing. There were improvements to make but nothing of any great consequence. It was a very different game from Ireland. There had been far more continuity, far more control and even though we had not dominated throughout we had ended up with our biggest winning margin against France for many years. We were in good heart.

INTERVIEW WITH DAVID SOLE

ROBERTSON: *Just like the Irish game you had problems at half-time because with a gale-force wind behind Scotland you only led 3–0. How worried were you?*

SOLE: I was really more frustrated than worried because just like the game in Dublin we had squandered several chances by missing penalty kicks and by failing to cash in on try-scoring opportunities after we had done the hard work by creating the chances. We should have been about 15 points up and that would have been a reasonable cushion but I still didn't feel too apprehensive at the end of the first half.

ROBERTSON: *What message did you put across in the half-time team talk?*

SOLE: I stressed that the biggest mistake we could make in the second half would be to become defensively minded because it would be pointless to try to sit on our lead as we didn't have a worth-while lead to sit on. I told the team we had to go and play as if we were six points down and had to fight our way back into the game. I emphasized the need to raise the pace of the game which we did.

ROBERTSON: *What did you feel was the turning point of the match?*

SOLE: I think there were two turning points. Firstly, the wind which had been very strong and right behind us in the first half, changed direction and blew not only more across the field in the second half but also with less strength. Secondly, a quarter of an hour into the second half Alain Carminati was sent off for deliberately stamping on John Jeffrey and, reduced to 14 men for the rest of the match, you could visibly see the French heads drop. We seized our chance and the team rallied instantly to produce a renewed surge which further disheartened the French. The French are never the same force at Murrayfield that they are in Paris and they seemed to lose their impetus.

ROBERTSON: *Apart from the Calcutta Cup game, was the second half against France the best 40 minutes of the six internationals of the season?*

SOLE: Yes, without a doubt. It was our positive play which left the French demoralized and credit must go to our vastly improved lineout play with Chris Gray outstanding, to the phenomenal tack-ling of the tight forwards in particular and the whole team in general and the excellent play of the back row in the loose where they were responsible for setting up good second-phase possession time and time again. Above all, the second half produced a great team effort.

John Jeffrey celebrates as Iwan Tukalo scores Scotland's final try against France

INTERVIEW WITH GAVIN HASTINGS

ROBERTSON: *Were you an anxious man at half-time with only a 3–0 lead?*

HASTINGS: Amazingly enough, I honestly wasn't all that worried although I knew we hadn't taken full advantage of the wind in the first half and we hadn't capitalized on all our scoring chances, but at least we had created several opportunities whereas France had not. The wind was strong but it was more sharp gusts than a prolonged help to us and even before half-time it was beginning to die down a little and it changed direction to blow more diagonally across the pitch rather than straight downfield. The fact is that France never mounted any really dangerous attacks in the first 40 minutes and they never threatened to break down our defence so I felt at half-time if the forwards continued to hold the edge in the set-pieces and kept on top in the loose and the backs tied up the midfield with aggressive defence, there was every reason to expect to maintain or even increase our lead.

ROBERTSON: *Did the sending-off of Carminati settle the issue?*

HASTINGS: No, I was quite confident France still would not have won even if he hadn't been sent off. We were comfortably containing the French in the second half even before the Carminati incident. Our forwards raised their effort and they won so much good quality possession I think the French were pretty demoralized even before they lost Carminati. You've got to remember their morale couldn't have been very high at the start of the match because they'd changed their team dramatically after their heavy defeat by England in Paris and with half the team altered, there was understandably a lack of continuity and cohesion in their play. There's no doubt they lacked their traditional creative play and a lot of credit must go to our pack because we outplayed them in the forward battle.

ROBERTSON: *What happened to Blanco, Lagisquet, Sella and Mesnel – their usual match-winners?*

HASTINGS: The simple answer is that our backs knocked them over whenever they even threatened to make a break. This was especially true of my brother Scott and Sean Lineen in the centre who completely snuffed out Sella and Mesnel – halting them in their tracks every time they tried to run. As Bill Beaumont said on BBC Television at the time, 'You don't get much change out of running straight at Scott Hastings and Sean Lineen.'

ROBERTSON: *Can you pick a couple of reasons why Scotland beat France?*

Gary Armstrong launches a Scottish attack featuring seven Scots players and virtually no French presence at all

HASTINGS: First of all our forwards outplayed them in the set pieces and our back row were much faster and reacted more quickly and decisively in the loose. With the tackling of the whole back division so tight, we severely restricted their running opportunities and by putting them under sustained pressure for 80 minutes, which they're not used to in the home Championship, they cracked. Some people were a bit critical of our performance afterwards but how many other sides have beaten France by a margin of 21 points in the last 15 years?

4. Wales v. Scotland

It was a poor game. Wales had made wholesale changes after the appointment of Ron Waldron from Neath as the new coach. Scotland were once again unchanged. Scotland dominated the set pieces but failed really to use their superiority to any great effect. Scotland led 10–3 at half-time. Armstrong broke around the front of a lineout to link with his forwards. The good support of Jeffrey and Sole created the try for Cronin. Infringements by Wales gave Craig Chalmers the opportunity to extend the Scottish lead. He duly accepted with two well-struck penalty goals. Thorburn missed three kicks at goal for Wales but was successful with the conversion of Emyr's try. It came from the best move of the match which started from a tap penalty on half-way. The ball moved through several pairs of Welsh hands before a deft switch by Mike Hall took the ball back the other way where it finally reached Emyr. The Swansea wing raced to the line for a fine try. Chalmers' third penalty goal was enough to keep Scotland in front.

Phil Davies of Wales and Scotland's Chris Gray and Paul Burnell indulge themselves in a 'Spot the Ball' competition

We were starting to feel confident. I think that the French game showed to the players that if they worked at something collectively, then it could be very effective. The lineout in that game was a very good example. We'd set out to impose a certain pattern and it paid off. The players like that, to think that they have deliberately brought something about. It gives them a sense of control.

That was the great strength of the side this year. The basic organization of the players was very sound and they had enough belief in themselves and the players around them to adapt to whatever circumstances arose. There was a real feeling of unity about them, unity of purpose and ideas. They felt comfortable with each other and so they felt comfortable in the games, no matter how tough the going got.

So the fact that we were now moving towards a position I'd never been in in my life, going for a second away win and going three up, did not unsettle them. They had faith that they could deliver. Once again a possible Grand Slam was never really entertained at this juncture. We always focus on the next opponents.

Wales had been humiliated by England. That concerned me. It might have given some people relief but I feared the backlash. I knew enough about their club rugby and had experienced the fervour of the Arms Park enough times to know that whatever Welsh side came out against us would be charged up, hell-bent on proving that what had happened at Twickenham was just a bad dream. They would be highly motivated. We would have to be highly disciplined. There was no doubt of that in my mind. So that was the one word at the top of my list of priorities for the Sunday session – CONTROL.

We had to try and dampen the excitement that would be in the air at Cardiff because if they got some early points on the board it would make it extremely difficult to get back in the game. Once again, that

is the difficulty of playing away from home. If things go against you early on then it can be so hard to re-establish yourself. We had to get control right from the start against Wales and not allow them any chance to settle.

It was a great help having an unchanged side. It was to turn out to be the first time ever that Scotland had fielded the same XV throughout and very grateful I was that we were able to do so. Your biggest obstacle is always injury and we were blessed not to suffer any at all. Any slight doubts about the form or suitability of a particular player was heavily outweighed by the benefit of having the same guys together all through. You start to achieve the cohesion and understanding that a club side has. Training sessions are much more efficient and productive because you can assume a basic level of understanding about what you are trying to achieve. And in the different units on the field you begin to see players react instinctively to each other. They anticipate better; they link better and a much closer team spirit develops. We duly picked the same XV against Wales.

I always have a general aim to try and shorten the sessions as the season goes on. The players themselves are in the middle of a very intense period, both physically and psychologically. They need rest if they can get it. You should by this stage be on the same wavelength in set-piece play. Obviously I throw in different routines to keep the players sharp and to meet specific needs, but generally the set play is by now well ordered.

The Sunday and Thursday work was all about control. On Sunday we were again in the dark about the composition of the Welsh XV because they had delayed selection. I figured that the game was going to be very hectic and that the Welsh pack would be quite heavy. I thought that we might look to control the ball in midfield, get there quickly, take the ball away again so that you've got the ball on the move and in the areas where you want it to be. That means that you avoid the messy contact situations where unexpected contact would make the ball difficult to control.

We did a lot of practice that Sunday on contact work. In fact we did all week, either against live opposition or by use of pads. We even did contact work on the Friday before, which is slightly unusual. Pads are a great way of simulating contact, just one person holding them as the players make a hit. The whole game of rugby is really about what happens on contact: how you control that contact and what is happening to the ball. If you can master that, you're in business. Of course there are still decisions to be made after that, but what happens in that moment of contact is absolutely vital.

One of our great strengths is that we can stay on our feet and ruck. Now if you can do that in numbers and you can ruck every situation, then it tends to take a lot of the frenetic activity out of the contact.

Scott Hastings passes to Tony Stanger just as Alan Bateman tackles him

The actual target in a ruck is moving in a very specific way. That was another means of trying to exert control and lessen the effect of the fanatical backing Wales were sure to get.

As it happens, the Welsh team selection didn't quite work out as I had anticipated. Rather than a heavy sort of pack, they had an extremely light front row. It seems they were also intent on running around a bit. That didn't worry me unduly because it suited our own style as long as we dictated exactly where the contact point would be – somewhere around outside centre was our plan. It also meant that we worked a bit harder in practice on set-piece play so that we could try and gain an advantage there. The lineout had gone very well against France so we were looking for a repeat of that.

The Thursday session was just over two hours long. Once again it was windy. It seems most of the season was to be played with a gale blowing somewhere or other. We'd coped with those conditions against France and we simply ran through the options available there. We were on the Murrayfield pitch itself that Thursday. It's a much quicker surface than the pitches outside, about a yard quicker I would say. Once you're inside the stadium as well you start to get a sense of atmosphere. It just makes the players concentrate that little bit more. Now that we knew the Welsh side, we talked about the possibilities. I noted that they had picked two open-side flankers in

Richie Collins ploughs forward into a navy blue reception committee

their team – Collins and Perego – and we worked a bit on attacking their blind side.

Friday morning was a bright, clear day. We had flown down from Scotland the previous afternoon. We were outside Cardiff at St Pierre in Chepstow. We were at it for an hour that morning, lineout being a prime consideration. I have a basic pattern for every session which involves warm-up, skill work, match patterns, wind-down. The content obviously varies according to the specific needs of the match ahead. The key thing is to try and get the balance right: making them work hard but not thinking that they're doing so much that they need a rest.

Friday afternoons, the players do what they want. Some relax in their rooms, others go for a stroll, whilst some might play snooker or whatever. I prefer to go out with the other coaches for a walk. In Edinburgh we go down into the town from the Braid Hills and have a cappuccino in a little coffee shop. In Chepstow we ambled round the

David Sole in the thick of battle in the Welsh match

golf course for about an hour and a half. It's always very relaxing, chatting about the game ahead as well as weighing up where we are with the team as a whole. The talking helps to order your thoughts. It's so important in those final hours to be as precise and concise as possible. The players are starting to switch into themselves and do not want too much to clutter their mind.

That Friday evening I took them through a few sequences from the French game on video as well as our last two encounters with Wales which had both been high-scoring.

As it turned out this was not a high-scoring affair. We simply did not get as much continuity as we wanted which was reflected in a very stop-start game. The ball, for a variety of reasons, got held in. I think there were probably only two or three times in the whole match when we actually managed to get the pace under control, work through the breakdowns and consider developing the play. The Welsh, as I suspected, were playing on a high which was evidenced by the frenetic nature of much of the game. That didn't really suit our intentions and we rarely came to terms with that.

The score was close but I never felt we were in any serious trouble. Even when the run of play was going against us, I was able to scan the field and see that everyone was in the right position. We were able to stay in the game even after Wales scored their try; there was a sense of organization about the side. We missed a couple of tackles early on in that movement which got us into trouble but had recovered well enough by the time Emyr went over in that he was being chased by three blue shirts. Had the line been another 10 yards further on, it might have been interesting.

We defended well for much of that match, although our touch kicking was too short at times. We won enough ball when Wales were pressing to have cleared our lines properly. We failed to do so. That period just before half-time when Wales were camped on our line was crucial. I think if Wales had scored then it would have been more dangerous than when they actually did score. They would have gone into half-time with their confidence up. As it was, it was Scotland who went in with their tails up; they had withstood all that pressure, which gave them great reassurance about their own defensive abilities.

The centres looked very firm throughout. Sean and Scott always work as a pair, so that whether they come rocketing up or are hanging off their man, it doesn't matter as long as they are doing it together. That sort of discipline and harmony ran throughout the side. A sense of organization and togetherness can only come from playing together. Most of the side had played the previous season; seven or eight of them had played in Australia for the Lions so you have this great sense of a shared purpose and understanding. One player wouldn't try to do something off his own bat which might upset the

Alan Bateman races through to set up Arthur Emyr for the only Welsh try of the match

rhythm elsewhere. There was always a collective awareness about them. Of course certain individuals stand out from time to time. John Jeffrey in this match I thought was outstanding. Damian Cronin took his try very well also. It was nice to see that the close control and inter-passing, which we had worked on in training so often, actually paid off. We've always worked a lot on unconventional passing in practice because you never know in a match just where the ball will be coming from, or how the space will be created. It's crucial that when you are under pressure you are still able to work the ball away. The All Blacks are masters at it.

Our tight scrummage against Wales was encouraging. We had

targeted the tight as an area where we might put pressure and inject some control. There was a sequence of play when we opted to re-scrummage rather than take the penalty offered. That was David Sole's decision and one which made some sense. We had a definite edge in the scrums and felt that we could drive over. Psychologically it was no bad thing either to underline your advantage. As it was we only finally got three points from a penalty, but we had drained Wales even further. David Sole said that his legs were absolutely shattered at the end of those scrummages, which shows the kind of pressure that can be exerted through tight scrummaging.

The mood in the dressing room afterwards was quite good. It had not been the greatest of spectacles but the players felt that they had never been under massive threat, that they had shown far more control in this match than they had against Ireland. They felt that they had been able to relieve pressure reasonably well. We didn't, though, put the pressure we wanted on Wales. We wanted to attack them quickly. We failed to do that. Our attacks were too long and drawn out, which didn't suit what we were trying to do. Of course once that starts happening in a match, it is very difficult to get it back. We didn't have control in attack. When we came to preparing for England, I used a detailed analysis of this match showing several examples of poor control – either the ball-carrier was not protected properly, or a loose ball was not tied in or there was no momentum in the drive. Players would often arrive at a loose situation and fall rather then step into it.

However we had won away from home again, for only the fourth time in over 50 years in Cardiff. We were now set for the showdown with England.

INTERVIEW WITH DAVID SOLE

ROBERTSON: *This was another close result with only one score in it. How near did Wales come to halting Scotland's winning run?*

SOLE: To be honest I always felt we were going to win though I was a little anxious that we were never able to draw two scores clear of Wales. The fact is we were on top early on, took the lead with the try from Damian Cronin and were in front for the rest of the game. I was confident throughout that our forwards were more than a match for the Welsh; and for once Wales did not have a genius in the mould of Jonathan Davies who could, even behind a beaten pack, turn a game upside down on his own by making or scoring a couple of brilliant tries or drop goals as Davies had done in the past. That is not to sug-

Kevin Phillips is the Welsh meat in a Scottish sandwich comprising Gary Armstrong and Craig Chalmers

gest it was an easy win because in fact it was a very hard, very physical battle up front in which we had the edge but could never afford to relax for a moment.

ROBERTSON: *Were you a little disappointed it wasn't a spectacular match?*

SOLE: No, not particularly. On my two previous Scotland–Wales games in Cardiff we played in two much better, far more spectacular games but on each occasion Scotland lost. This time it wasn't a classic but at least we won and found ourselves three-quarters of the way to a Grand Slam.

ROBERTSON: *What were the key elements in the victory?*

SOLE: The single most important factor was our domination of the scrums. This was significant in its own right, but also it led to our control in the open and in other areas. We knew when the Welsh changed the emphasis of their pack selection with their new coach they would try to repeat his club, Neath's, mobility with Wales. Their front row are not renowned for their scrummaging ability and we decided to take full advantage of that. Paul Burnell was set two tasks. Firstly, to attack and out-scrummage his opposite number Brian Williams and secondly, to tackle Kevin Phillips every time he ran with the ball from a short penalty. He accomplished both tasks superbly. Damian Cronin had a great game in the lineout and the loose and with our pack sweeping everything before them the back row and the half-backs had a field day. To give you an example of our scrummaging superiority we often only put seven forwards into the scrum, leaving John Jeffrey standing off waiting to drive back any Welsh back-row or scrum-half break. This worked a treat. When Wales had several scrums near our line in one burst in the first half, their number eight Mark Jones picked up every time and set off for our line only to be rocketed backwards on every occasion by John Jeffrey. And our relentless, grinding scrummaging took the sting out of the mobility of their forwards leaving them leg-weary by the end. Our scrummaging laid the foundations of our victory.

INTERVIEW WITH GAVIN HASTINGS

ROBERTSON: *Did you feel this win against Wales was a bit easier than the score might suggest?*

HASTINGS: I don't think it's ever easy to beat Wales in Cardiff and this was a very hard match but at no stage did I ever fear we were going to lose. I thought we were under much more pressure against Ireland and France and though the home crowd were passionately behind their team, the Welsh were fairly predictable and didn't show a great deal of originality in trying to break our pretty well-organized defensive system. Their best hope of points would have been if we had given away a few penalties but we produced a very disciplined performance and Wales didn't have many opportunities to score. We never looked like cutting loose and running up a big score but I think we always looked as if we would win because we had the better pack on the day; we kept a tight tactical control on the game and even if it wasn't an overwhelming win judging by the final score, it was nonetheless well deserved. We were confident right the way through.

ROBERTSON: *What made you so confident?*

HASTINGS: All sorts of things really. We had a settled side full of experienced players with four international victories behind us, while Wales were recovering from three successive defeats and had a re-shaped team including loads of changes and a new coach. It was interesting when we lined up before the kick-off and looked at the Welsh side. Usually the Scots, especially the forwards, expect to be smaller and lighter than the opposition but in Cardiff it was different this year. I could hardly see one of their team who was any taller than me and I thought then we had to have a great chance of winning because our pack would probably come out on top and with our emphasis all season on mobility we were bound to have the upper hand in the open. And I think that sort of confidence spread right through our team. After all, for that match we had eight 1989 British Lions in our side, the Welsh had only two.

ROBERTSON: *Finally, if you were asked which one aspect of the game made the biggest difference between the teams, what would you say?*

HASTINGS: Experience. There's no doubt we had a far more experienced side and experience counts for an enormous amount in international rugby. This is one reason why we can now look forward optimistically to the World Cup because almost all of our experienced players should still be playing right through 1991.

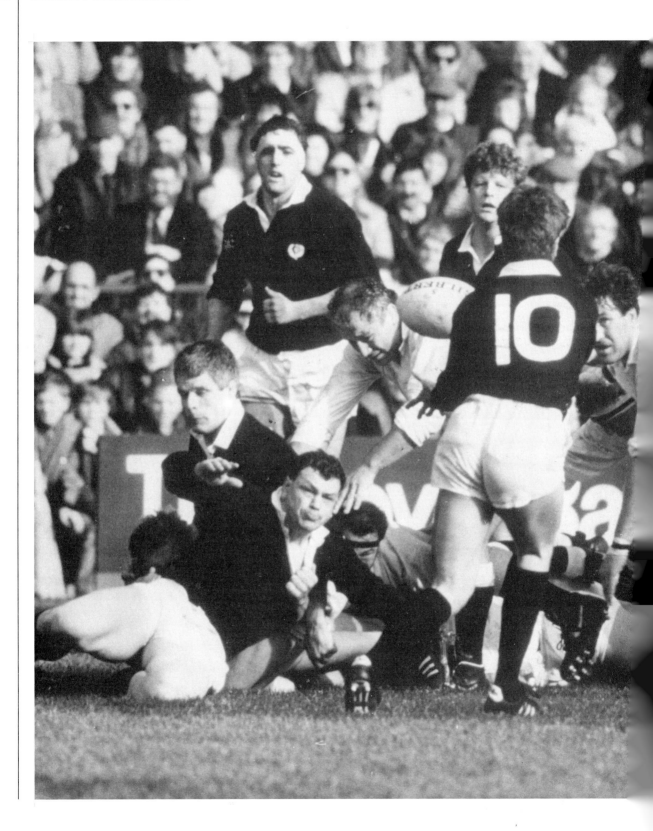

5. The Royal Bank of Scotland *Scotland v. England*

It was a very tight, tense match. Having received a rapturous welcome from a packed Murrayfield, Scotland made an impressive start driving England backwards in the first 10 minutes. Craig Chalmers was able to kick two penalties in this opening spell with the wind at his back. Five minutes later, though, England were back in the game. A midfield drive by number eight Mike Teague produced a good ball for England on half-way. Richard Hill moved the ball on quickly and Jeremy Guscott was able to glide 30 metres to the line. Scotland resisted some heavy England pressure during which England elected to run several penalties. A Chalmers penalty just before half-time gave Scotland a 9–4 half-time lead. Against the wind in the second half, Scotland could not have had a better start. Jeffrey broke from a scrum on half-way, fed Armstrong who drew two men before delivering to Gavin Hastings. His kick to the line was brilliantly caught on the bounce by Tony Stanger who crossed for a fine try. Hodgkinson's penalty 15 minutes into the half narrowed the gap but it was not enough. Scotland had won the game and had taken only their third Grand Slam in history.

Kenny Milne plays the role of make-shift scrum-half to feed Craig Chalmers

I was now entering into a unique period in my rugby life. The words 'Grand Slam' were first mentioned at the team meeting after the Wales match. We got back to the hotel, dropped the bags in the foyer and found a room. Any old room would do – somewhere to have a quick, instinctive assessment of what had just happened. This time though, although several points were made about the performance against Wales, the players' minds were already elsewhere. Murrayfield, England and the Grand Slam.

There was a bit of a buzz about the meeting. The prospect was fantastic. No British sides had ever been in this situation before – the last game, both unbeaten, a Grand Slam for the winner. The game was to be at Murrayfield to boot and already the heart was beginning to race. Conversation at dinner that Saturday evening just kept coming back round to it. I spent most of the time chatting to Robin Chartres and Derrick Grant about the next two weeks and a few ideas about how to cope with England tactically were already spinning around my head. We'd mentioned earlier to the players that we would ease down on the volume of training and go for more refined speed work. We told the players that the next two weeks would be probably unique in their rugby lives and that they had to put their minds to it. Not that they needed any encouragement.

I drove back to Leeds from Cardiff the next morning. It was nice just to have three or four hours to order a few thoughts. It was all motorway and not too busy, so I began to tune in to the fortnight ahead. It was just as well I had those few hours to myself on the drive back for it proved to be one of the rare occasions when I had proper time to think. The phone barely stopped ringing in the next two weeks.

I'd chatted to a few of the senior players on Saturday evening – David Sole, Finlay, JJ, Gavin – and we decided that between us we would field the media enquiries. There was pressure enough on the younger boys without having to cope with the barrage of journalists and television crews that were likely to descend upon them. I don't think any one of us realized, however, just how great the level of interest would be. I got home from school at six o'clock Monday evening and was on the phone until eleven o'clock. It was only then that I was able to get down to some proper rugby work – studying videos and preparing notes. It was the same pattern all week. The midnight oil was well and truly burned in our house that week. I hardly saw my wife, Judy, or two children, Heather and Robert, all week. When I returned from Edinburgh after selection on Tuesday, Judy gave me a list as long as her arm of people who had called. The constant ringing made her scream with frustration one night, as it literally never stopped.

I simply turned up for work at school that week. I certainly didn't have my mind properly on it. I would try and tidy up a few things in

Paul Burnell arrests PC Paul Ackford for loitering with intent

the afternoon before heading for home and the usual round of local press and TV before speaking to the nationals on the phone.

I suppose I could have turned down the requests but it wasn't my way. You have a responsibility to the game and you have to try and present everything in the best light. On the Lions tour I'd always tried to make time for the press, inviting them to every training session just so that they would understand what we were trying to do.

I figured that if I was handling as much as I could then it would reduce the pressure on those who really mattered – the players. In fact, I never buy a newspaper so I never saw what was written. I prefer being in glorious isolation, except on Sundays. I don't have much spare time anyway and it might only end up with me getting upset, so what's the point. I use the Ceefax service on the television to keep up with the news about teams and squads and I find that is enough. I know the players are much more avid about what is written in the papers. In a way you're always searching for an accolade. They're not so keen to buy a paper when they've lost. I was the same when I played. It's different being a coach because you know what you want to do and you don't need it to be confirmed or rejected by someone else. People think differently about the game so there's no point worrying about someone else's opinion. It is an unnecessary diversion.

I knew that most of the English press would base their comments around England. That made sense because that is where they are based and where most of their readership lies. It didn't concern me. I've never been too worried about how critical people are. The Lions tour had taught me a bit about how intense some papers could be. There wasn't exactly a witch hunt after we had lost the First Test but you could sense that some people were desperate to close in on us. But as I'd always tried to be very open about intentions and the way we were trying to play the game, they couldn't pretend to be too wise after the event.

It was all very tiring but just part of the whole experience. It was going to be an historical encounter and all this interest was part of it. As long as I was able just to shut myself off for those couple of late hours every night and get my preparation done, then I wasn't too worried about it. Desperately tired, but not worried.

There wasn't really too much new to consider about the match. By this stage of a successful season, many things are fairly settled. It was just a matter of getting our things in order and saying, as we'd done with every other side, right, now it's England, what are our priorities? The video analysis centred on England's win in Paris and a little bit of their victory against Ireland. I hadn't bothered with them at all before this juncture. I'd seen their win in Paris because it was the same weekend as I was at home ill in Leeds. It was only on video, though, that I was able to dissect it. England had been impressive in that game. There was no doubt about it. I didn't really

Damian Cronin takes an excellent two-handed catch

concern myself too much with their win over Wales. Wales had not really come up to scratch that day and had made it quite easy for England. I would have torn my hair out if Scotland had done some of the things they did that day. But in Paris, England had won the match and won it well. They were playing a much more fluid game and you could see how some of the players who had been on the Lions tour were performing. They were playing with a great deal of confidence, and I had a lot of respect for them. England had in fact been under pressure themselves but dealt with it. That's when you see how a team really operates – when they are under pressure.

Of course you can't direct your comments to your own team like this. There's no sense in building up a picture of how invincible the opposition might be. The idea was to assess their strengths and

weaknesses and then incorporate these ideas into how we wanted to play the game. We had to channel everything into a positive framework. Jim Telfer focuses on lineout and back-row whereas I'll look at the links and continuity. We spent some time on the phone ourselves that week but, by and large, we knew where we were going. Often the coaches will have spent much of that season, at dinners, at selection and at training itself, discussing Scotland's game.

We had to look at England now as we always used to look at France. If things were done badly, you could safely assume that England would score. That was the way it used to be with France. If we weren't right, then England would be. Everything was geared to that end. We had given Wales too much space. If we gave that to England, then they would exploit it and we would be out of the game. It was as clear-cut as that.

I took that line at all the training sessions. I aimed for intensity. No unforced errors, and always be aware of the calibre of the side we were playing. Richard Hill had matured; Rob Andrew had the confidence to dictate and make the side operate; Rory Underwood was in great form. All round they had several arms which they could use to score.

When we gathered in Edinburgh on that Saturday evening, the four coaches sat down for dinner and went through quite methodically the various aspects of the game. The lineout had gone well but it had to get better. It had to be as well organized as we could possibly make it, just to give us a 50–50 chance. England were strong in that department, as I knew full well from the Lions tour. Scrummage work had to be spot on and we had to close England down at every opportunity. Sounds simple really.

Sunday's session was a good session because a lot of the players had decided not to play that weekend. The back row had decided 10 minutes after the Welsh game not to risk playing. They knew that they would never get a chance like it again. So they were ultra fit, ultra fresh for the Sunday session. The actual advantages in terms of physical performance from not playing might really only have been negligible, but psychologically they felt much better. They'd pared down the heavy leg work in training so that made them feel a lot sharper. It also allowed us to do things with a much greater intensity. Everything was done against live opposition so as to get used to not making mistakes. We were out for about two and a quarter hours.

We knew England had a lot of control in the set-pieces. That was where they had exerted pressure against France. There had been a lot of talk about bringing in Iain Milne – The Bear – to bolster our scrummage. As it happens I couldn't have been happier with the way we had performed in the scrummage. Paul Burnell had come along superbly all season and our scrummage work that week in training just got better and better. It showed in the game itself, I think.

We had a full session on Wednesday evening. Jim Telfer took the forwards whilst I was inside for about 45 minutes with the backs. We ran through a couple of incidents from videos and then went outside. It was one of the best sessions I've ever taken. Everything was so slick, so fast, so disciplined, so error-free that I pulled them up early. We only had 25 minutes. There was a keenness and a ripple about everything.

Meanwhile Jim was also finishing early. The forwards were throwing themselves at the scrummage machine with all the weight on, though not recklessly. Jim said that they were as technically accomplished as he had ever seen them. A session like that did confidence no harm at all, I can tell you.

On Thursday we spent a bit more time talking about tactics, about how to put pressure on England. We knew of course that we had to

Tony Stanger and Jeremy Guscott become entangled as the ball eludes both of them and John Jeffrey as well

compete in every phase. They had shown, particularly against France, that once they were in control it was very difficult to break that pattern. We had to get in amongst them. The session was a bit longer than I would have liked, about two and a half hours, and it was a bit stop-start. I deliberately finished with two non-stop lengths just to put the pace in there again. I was a bit aware that we'd been out a long time. But it was right that we talked things through, that we changed things just a little to keep the players on their toes.

Once again we put a few new patterns into the pre-ordained lineout blocks. We knew that we had to try and move around a lot and keep the ball away from their two big men. Change the length, change the jumpers, whatever. In fact we felt we had one more natural jumper in the line than England. Chris Gray, Damian Cronin and the back row are all club jumpers. England only really had four. So it was up to Kenny Milne to find that extra jumper.

Lineout ball was absolutely crucial. The half-backs could both control a game so it was vital to put pressure on England by denying them their normal platform. However, it was not just a matter of being destructive. We also had to be positive. We wanted to take the game to them as well. I felt we had the potential to put the ball through the hands. In fact the way we started in the match showed just that. We went at them with a superbly aggressive and attacking attitude.

I was determined to keep the routine exactly as before. If I changed it I felt I would be putting pressure on the players by emphasizing that this game was different. I consciously kept the pattern of the sessions the same as well as the way I addressed them. Obviously their own training was more intense but that was to be expected. Intensity was going to be a key word in the build-up. If we could operate in that atmosphere, in which everything might be happening half a yard quicker than they had experienced before, then we might be in business. There was to be nothing loose at all. England had dominated their opponents because they had been allowed to dictate the pace. We had to change that.

Everything was geared to getting everyone in the right place at the right time. Finlay had said after the Lions tour just how impressed he had been by the upper body strength of the English forwards. That meant we had to make sure we had men at the breakdown in numbers and in the right place.

We had a big lunch at Murrayfield that Thursday afternoon. It was a late finish, about 2.30, so we had only a short time to kill before the evening meeting at seven o'clock. Most of the players just wandered back up to the Braid Hills and played pool or rested in their rooms. I was relieved, now that we had actually got to this stage of the preparations, that we were all together and working. I had been pretty churned up for the last ten days. Normally I sleep very

John Jeffrey prepares to tackle Richard Hill with Derek White checking that nothing goes wrong

soundly but I'd tossed and turned nearly every night and had been waking up much earlier. It was perhaps due to the fact that I was working later and the phone was forever on the go. When I woke at six in the morning that was it. My mind was so active that I just had to get up and get on with something. I used the scribble board in the kitchen a lot during that time, jotting down anything that came into my head, just in case it might be relevant later.

I was anxious, though, not to convey my hyperactivity to the players. I deliberately controlled my voice when speaking to them. I avoided anything out of the ordinary even though I felt anything but ordinary. There was a lot of laughing and joking amongst the squad,

particularly from the senior players. I'm sure that was a release of tension in many ways, but it helped keep the anxiety level down.

It was of course a very special match and there was no way that you could really pretend otherwise. However I was very confident that although the match would be tense the atmosphere would be healthy. The Scottish and English players had got on very well during the Lions tour; they had an awful lot of respect as well as feeling for each other. I knew there was no danger of anyone going over the top.

We knew there was more to come out of us, that we had not performed to our full potential. The players were all quite self-critical which was a good sign. They knew what they had to do to improve. By Friday morning you could feel a sharper edge. I remember sitting them down before they went out to train that morning at Boroughmuir. I told them that they were in a unique position, one which I'd never been in before. 'You are a unique Scottish side,' I said, 'so go out and enjoy this session and enjoy the attention of all those who have come along to watch. They come to watch a bit of history. Enjoy that experience for tomorrow will be a unique day.'

The session, even though it was windy, was spot on. There was only one lineout throw which went to the wrong place and even that was picked up by someone else. It missed Chris Gray, it missed Damian, but JJ snaffled it and had it whipped out to Gary Armstrong in no time. The reactions were all very sharp. The level of concentration was tremendous. The players were criss-crossing in their small group, passing, and there was not a ball out of place. You could see that even the casual observer was impressed. We didn't divide up as we normally do after these warm-up exercises but went straight in to the team phase. I said that we would just do five lengths and that was all. David Sole did the last couple of lengths. That was it: 35 minutes. But it was enough. I wanted to call them up a little bit short just so that they were eager to get at it. But they were ready, mentally and physically. There was no doubt about it.

The Friday afternoon followed the usual format. Jim Telfer in fact goes back on Thursday night to teach on the Fridays. He's a headmaster in Hawick. He's back up for the meeting at 6 p.m. I wandered down into Morningside with the other coaches for a cappuccino and just chatted until five o'clock. It's our little Friday afternoon ritual. As we get nearer the game I'll try to withdraw. The players need to take over. The forwards and the backs both had a huddle in the bar early that evening – just a drink and a talk about what lay before them. At the team meeting we looked at bits and pieces that had gone well that season, against France and Wales. Sometimes I might use charts on a Friday evening but I decided to keep things as simple as possible. We just had a general free discussion about what we were going to try to do, reinforcing everything

Did anyone see which way the ball went?

we had done in training.

The Braid Hills is a good place to stay because it is very quiet, only about 15 minutes from Murrayfield, and has a very homely feel to it which the players enjoy. We had stayed out at Dunblane before the Romanian game but it was not the right feel. We had been scheduled to stay there for England but I asked for a change. Everything had to feel just right.

The players either went off to the cinema to watch 'Born on the Fourth of July' or stayed in the hotel where Iwan Tukalo and Scott Hastings had organized half a dozen videos. Everyone was back in place for hot chocolate and biscuits at half past ten. It was all

exactly as normal. Everyone seemed quite relaxed. I slept well that night.

Saturday morning is always the worst period. You're really only killing time. It was windy. I had phoned Murrayfield the day before and asked if we could come down for a short session with the kickers if it were windy. The problem is of course getting into the place on a Saturday morning, particularly as Her Royal Highness would be in attendance. We had to get special passes.

I never realized just how much goes on. It was a hive of activity. Security was already there so if we'd not had those passes we would not have got in. The TV crews were all busy rigging the equipment, the caterers were busy setting up their stalls and the like. There was already a real buzz about the place, even inside the dressing rooms. The sniffer dogs were there as we walked in, with mirrors looking under all the benches. We were on the field by about 9.20 – Craig, Gary, Gavin and myself. We'd never done this before a game, but after the French game when it had also been very windy I thought it would be a good thing to get an early feel of the conditions. It's a strange wind now at Murrayfield. When I played the east side was all terracing and you could actually read the wind. Now it's a bit like Twickenham used to be with the wind swirling about. The boys just put up some big kicks from all parts of the ground, just to gauge how the wind was behaving in that particular corner. They could then work out whether they needed to kick high or low, long or short. It only took about 20 minutes but it was very useful. In fact it almost backfired on us: Gavin had walloped a ball with his full power which got caught in the wind. It veered savagely away and caught Craig full belt on the nose. There was blood everywhere. It was a good job there were no photographers around to catch that one.

A few folk came out to watch us practise. The head groundsman Bill Elwood was having kittens in case we ruined his surface. They were still doing some cutting at that stage, trimming the surface, which is fabulous, down to the right level.

By the time we got back to the hotel is was mid-morning. We did the usual things. We went out for a quick loosener on the lawns at the side of the hotel. The forwards did some lineout work and the backs some quick passing. It helps get the feel of things as well as killing time. The hotel is very busy on an international morning with supporters checking in and people popping by to wish us good luck. You're very aware that things are building up to a climax. We have separate chats, then a team meeting before an early lunch at 11.30. Players eat anything from Mars bars to scrambled eggs to toast and soup. Each to his own. The schedule was all a bit earlier than usual because we were being presented to Her Royal Highness. I like to give the players an hour between lunch and departure just so that they have time to get themselves right. They might clean boots, read

Mike Teague drives forward as John Jeffrey and Derek White prepare to meet force with force

a paper or even lie down. Whatever they need to do to get in the right frame of mind, they need time to do it.

I had just five minutes with them before we got on the bus. I tried to distance myself and talk about how I was feeling. I'd had letters from Scots all over the world who all knew that this was a big occasion. I told the players that these Scots, wherever they were in the world, would be thinking of only one little patch this afternoon. That was what these players had already achieved. They were already special to those people. They had drawn us all as a nation together. They had to take that on the field with them. I knew how much this match meant to these folk because I'd spent most of my life outside Scotland. My father had always made me aware of how important it was to be Scottish. In fact it was brought home to me when I was out in Hong Kong for the Sevens a month later. The Scottish manager of the Hilton told me that he'd had a huge screen up that night and had everyone in to an enormous party.

Of course there's a crucial balance to be struck here. There's no point winding players up so tight that they freeze on you. Or getting them get so pumped up that they lose control. Balance is everything. A player has to be almost schizophrenic. He has to be so cool, calm and collected tactically yet he has to send his body physically into a maelstrom. It's peculiar really. So intense physically yet so detached

mentally. That's the frame of mind you're aiming for. That last hour before the game is very important because the adrenalin is in full flow and it's crucial to maintain cool heads and clear thoughts.

We left the Braid Hills at 12.50. On the bus at 1.00. The players were fairly quiet at this point. That's normal, for they are beginning to withdraw into themselves. It's the same in the changing room. They all get to the stage of getting on to the field in their own way. You leave them to it. You can't expect them to do what you want or even do a collective thing together. You have to respect that. I'm no tub-thumper, nor is David Sole, so perhaps that helps to keep the passions at the right level.

The coach ride to Murrayfield took about 15 minutes. The boys sang, 'Flower of Scotland' which was to be sung a few more times before the day was out. They don't always sing. It just depends if it feels right. It felt right. JJ tends to be the one that gathers them together. I tend to stay quiet and away from the players. I was fairly uptight and emotional and that's the last thing I wanted to convey to the players. It's a peculiar position. You've spent so much time thinking about and planning the match and now you can't do a thing about it. You come as close as six inches to the touchline, but unless you actually cross it, you're not fully there.

We arrived at 1.15. We were due out at 2.00 for the Royal presentation. I'd deliberately got them to the ground quite late so they wouldn't be hanging around too much, using up energy by fretting. I walked around the dressing room, having a quiet word with one or two individuals. Of course there's nothing left to say. I'm just doing it as a release for my own nervous energy. David Sole is to the fore at this point. There was a good strong sense of purpose in the air. No one was too wound-up or too on edge. They knew that they were going to have to perform as they had never performed before. It felt as if they might do just that.

The slow walk out of the tunnel was talked about the night before. Finlay Calder had pointed out that it had been tried before – when he was captain of the Lions before the First Test against Australia. 'Do you remember,' said Finlay, 'we got walloped?' It was of course different on home soil. It was the right thing to do because there was just the right feeling amongst the players themselves. The senior players had been tremendous in the last hour of the build-up, helping to settle the nerves of the younger guys, making sure they never got too uptight. Those that need to get really psyched up do it themselves. Everyone is on the move in those last 10 minutes. They all have a sweat on, are all locked in to the battle ahead. They all tend to talk to each other whilst David Sole just organizes a few last things. The attitude was just right. Out they went and what a welcome they got.

The Princess Royal with her children Peter and Zara being introduced to David Sole and the Scottish players

Jim Telfer and I in fact missed the entrance on to the field. We had left the changing room and gone the other way down the tunnel and up through a back door to the stand. Well, I'd never heard a noise like it. We both just looked at each other. You knew exactly what had just happened. I felt a real rush of emotion. Normally you're aware of the shouts and the cheering but this was just incredible, such an intense wall of noise. Bill McLaren told me afterwards that it really took him by surprise, he got a real lump in the throat. Luckily for him, there was no real need for any words. The noise just kept rising and rising. I thought it was never going to stop. It was quite magnificent.

It was now just a question of who got the bounces, who got in there first, where the ball went and who reacted the better. The first 10 minutes decided it to my mind. We got a good catch from Rob Andrew's kick-off. Gavin could have kicked a wee bit longer than he did. It was England's lineout but we won it. It went over the top, Finlay flicked it up, along it went from Craig to Sean Lineen. He ran 15 yards, hit the England centre and was promptly driven on another 10 yards by the pack who had come thundering in behind. We got a penalty and England hadn't even touched the ball.

Craig missed it but even from the drop-out we were on the front foot again. The next lineout went our way, the next scrum went up in the air and England realized that they had got a game on their hands. I think after that first scrummage Jeff Probyn knew that they had to stay down low. It wasn't our intention to put the scrum down at all. If there is a twist or a turn in anyone's shoulders, then with all that pressure coming through, it's bound to go down. You can't claim it's deliberate; it's just that if the shoulders are not square, then it will happen.

After that we got another penalty which Finlay took on the charge. He was hit hard by Micky Skinner, but crucially didn't go down. The whole pack once again drove in behind and shunted 15 yards. It's a huge psychological boost to a side when that happens. To boot we got a penalty at the end of the drive and Craig kicked the goal. Three points up and England had barely touched the ball. The same pattern continued for the next five minutes. We were positive, concerted and controlled. We took the ball at England, made ground and forced them into errors. Another penalty in the tenth minute was successfully kicked by Craig: 6–0 and what had England been able to do so far? I'm a terrible spectator at the best of times but even I felt quite happy after that opening.

It was important that we took the wind first. In a game as big as this one it is vital to establish yourself early on and likewise to deny the opposition any platform. That had been our game plan for England in any case, so it was all working out well. We wanted them to feel a bit of pressure. We wanted to dictate the pace of the game. We wanted to get early points on the board, something that England had

Craig Chalmers lands a vital early penalty for Scotland

*Damian Cronin secures possession as
the Scottish support heavily
outnumbers the English*

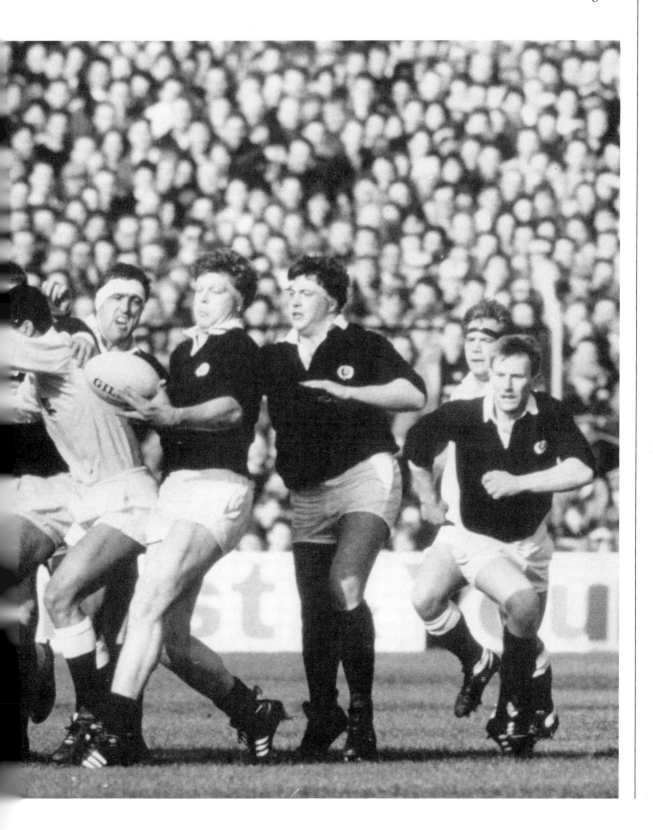

managed to do in their games.

I knew that we couldn't sustain that sort of pressure. But we had prepared ourselves to expect pressure, so that when it came, we wouldn't panic. It came a few minutes later when Jerry Guscott chipped for the corner but we managed to bundle the ball into touch. We won a crucial lineout decision on our own line. That happened throughout the game. Under pressure we did not crack. Such staunch defence lifts the one side and deflates the other.

The lineout variations we had pre-planned were working well. Finlay had come in at the last second to take a good ball at the front. I was very pleased with the lineout because England really are a formidable lineout side. Paul Ackford, who was on the Lions tour, really has put front jumping on to a new plane. I have the highest regard for him.

England's try in the 15th minute did knock us back a bit. However it was as expected, in a way. We had said beforehand that if they were given a bit of space then they would exploit it. We gave them space and they scored. It was not planned and those are the dangerous occasions. The ball had not come right and England had gone the opposite way. Scott Hastings had a word with the other threequarters: 'Defence has got to be absolutely spot-on. We must be alert at all times . . .' And they were for the rest of the match. It was an incredible display of defence because the pace of the game was so intense.

England put us under heavy pressure for the next 10 minutes. But we held. Many people have criticized England for not taking their kicks at goal during that period but I could see the logic in it. For that first scrummage we were down to seven men. But even after that they felt they could get a score and they are the people in the best position to know. I felt that perhaps there was more than one person making the decisions but even so, you want players to communicate. From our point of view it gave us a real lift to withstand that assault. Add to that Craig's third penalty five minutes from half-time and we went into the interval in a good position. Craig has done really well with his kicking this season. He is so accurate from 35 metres or so, just coolly chipping them over. Old head on young shoulders really.

I had already munched my way through several packets of sweets by half-time – chewing, talking, fretting up in the stand alongside Jim Telfer. I knew that the first quarter of an hour of the second half would decide it. We were against the wind and I was hoping that we could do as we had done against France when we put them back into their own half from the kick-off. Well, when our kick went out on the full and we had to come back to the middle for an English scrummage, my head dropped a little. Little did I know.

Tony Stanger's try was a superbly executed one a minute later. England did nothing wrong after the initial mistake of knocking on.

Micky Skinner and Mike Teague protect the ball as Chris Gray tries to step between them

Gary Armstrong drew two men in beautifully, Gavin's kick ahead was inch perfect and the way Tony plucked the ball from the air – it helps being six foot two – was terrific. It wasn't a scrambled affair. We'd created that one and England were shocked. They knew now that it was a long way back into the match and that if they gave us an inch of space, we too were capable of exploiting it.

I never felt the game was in the bag, though, until the closing minutes. I knew that it would be nip and tuck all the way through. But I also knew that our defence was as good, if not better, than anyone else's in the Championship. The great thing about much of our defence was that it was attacking defence. Time and again we drove at them. We didn't just hold on desperately but knocked them backwards. Will Carling was driven back 10 yards at one point; Gary Armstrong caught Richard Hill in possession, Finlay walloped in and we're away downfield again. It was defence to win ball, not just to defend. Everything was positive, dynamic.

We looked completely on top of the situation. No one was flagging, no one was panicking, no one was out of position. Rob Andrew kicked superbly that half, pinning us back on the 22 time and again. The support was a big factor in this half as well. Every time we cleared our lines a ripple of applause would turn into a huge wave of cheering right round the ground. Any 50–50 decision which went our way from the referee was greeted as if we had won the Championship. Everyone was following every little thing. No one was up in the stands drinking whisky and just having a good time. All eyes were on the game. It was a tremendous atmosphere. The last 10 minutes went quickly even though my heart missed a few beats when Richard Hill almost got away. We played a couple of minutes' injury time and then – whoosh – that was it. It was all over. Relief, total relief. Joy, amazement, pride – who knows what the emotions were? We were hugging each other, slapping backs, all around the committee box it was bedlam. You just couldn't take it all in.

We somehow found our way down to the dressing room. Jim Telfer and I found ourselves on our own in there. Where had the team got to? They were across in the other room, in fact, already in front of the TV cameras. It was all pretty chaotic. Finlay was completely choked and I must say I wasn't far behind him. I kept thinking 'Hang on, it's another of those dreams that have kept me awake for the last fortnight.' But there it was. It had been one hell of a match. Not open, flowing rugby but, as the whole of Murrayfield will tell you, Scottish or English, that didn't matter, it had been so intense that you were just rooted to the spot by it all.

Back in the dressing room, there were mixed scenes. Some were very quiet – Gary Armstrong, JJ – others just had a drink and slumped on the bench to let it all sink in. No one was really whooping it up. They had no energy left. You'd expect them to have been over

The happy smiles tell the whole story – Grand Slam number three for Scotland

the moon, shouting and cheering, but it was very similar to the Lions victory. There was just a quiet, satisfied feel to it. A lot was made about the fervid nationalism of the whole day. Although being Scottish and very proud of it was obviously important, there was no pre- or post-match ranting about putting it over the English. For a start, that would have been the wrong mental attitude to adopt because the players would probably have lost control. Secondly, the players had too much respect for their opponents for any of that. It was the desire of the underdog which motivated them.

The next few hours after the match were a swirl. Will Carling came in and offered his congratulations; Roger Uttley also put his head round the door. I popped out to the back of the stand and met up with my wife, Judy, and the two kids. Off to the tea-room; off to the press conference; off to the committee room. It was all one big merry-go-round of smiling faces, back-slapping, TV lights and microphones. As we went out to the bus there were still hundreds milling around. Up went that roar again. On the bus there were TV cameras, the boys were all singing and it was just all pure enjoyment.

I didn't think the Scottish players would ever get big-headed about it all. They're not that sort. Certainly there was no real crowing in victory that evening. They're all too down to earth for that. Little things keep your feet on the ground. As is the custom, we all had a quick drink in a pub near the hotel before going on to the President's reception dinner. I had one other task to perform, though. The kids were hungry so it was over the road into the Pizza Hut, black tie and all, and queue up for a Special with all the trimmings.

That night was a good night. It would have been a surprise if it hadn't been. Roger Uttley and I chatted through dinner; I spoke to several of the English players I knew. Brian Moore was perhaps the most disappointed but they were all very chivalrous in defeat. That's the great thing about the game really. It sounds a cliché, but the reality is still true. Hard on the pitch; great friends off it. Long may it be like that.

There's always a slight air of anti-climax after events like this, as if you are waiting for something else to happen. The next morning, or in fact the same morning for we had barely been to bed, the press were round for yet more photographs. It was then that tales came through of how people had been celebrating all over Scotland and how much it meant to them all. Norman Mair of *The Scotsman* told me that it had been like VE Day on the streets. The scores had even been relayed through to all the soccer grounds which is saying something in Scotland.

We drove home that morning to Leeds, stopping at Berwick *en route*. Cars full of English supporters were passing us all the time, shouting and waving if they recognized us. Shouting nice things, I might add! Home to Leeds that evening and there was yet another photographer on the doorstep. Would it never end, I thought?

There again, I suppose I didn't really want it to end. It had been a great season.

INTERVIEW WITH DAVID SOLE

ROBERTSON: *In the build-up to the Calcutta Cup game, did you agree that England deserved to be hot favourites to win?*

SOLE: Yes I did, because if you look at our respective performances against the other three sides in the Championship they had unquestionably played better in all three. They had scored 83 points whilst we had only managed to score 47 points. They had scored 11 tries in those three games to our five. They had looked really impressive whilst we had occasionally struggled.

ROBERTSON: *Did you think you had any major advantages going into the game?*

SOLE: Yes, we did have a few important things in our favour. Firstly, and perhaps the most significant point of all, we were playing at home and that was a huge bonus. Secondly, I thought we had a younger, perhaps fitter and certainly faster, more mobile set of tight forwards. And we had one crucial major advantage in our back division and that was at full-back where Gavin Hastings is now the best in the world, equally outstanding in attack and defence. Obviously, there were other areas where England were very strong but at least we had certain identifiable strengths and they had certain potential weaknesses. Also England had a real disadvantage with a four-week break from their Welsh match to the Murrayfield game whereas we kept the adrenalin pumping in our two-week gap between Cardiff and Murrayfield.

ROBERTSON: *What then was the Master Plan?*

SOLE: We were confident we could hold England in the scrummage but we knew we would have to introduce a great deal of variety to our lineout play which we did. It worked really well and we only rarely used an orthodox seven-man line with the locks jumping to two and four as a variation rather than as the norm. Enjoying our share at the set-pieces we determined to use our greater mobility to best advantage by increasing the pace and tempo of the game as much as we possibly could. We had to play flat out for 80 minutes and we did. The older, slower English tight forwards did tire first and when they took several tapped penalties near the end and gave the ball to Paul Rendall, all he was able to do was to turn round on the spot to set up the maul – there was no energy left for a ferocious flat-out charge at our line. We wanted to cut off their supply of ball if at all possible and if they did win possession to spoil and make it as poor quality as possible and then if it did reach the back division to sit on top of them, put them constantly under the maximum pressure and rattle in the tackles. Specifically we wanted Gary Armstrong to harry Richard Hill the whole time and make life as difficult as possible for him. The theme was to tackle everything that moved above grass level in an England shirt.

ROBERTSON: *What was the key to the success of this plan?*

SOLE: Quite simply, the fact that we did not let up, relax or break our concentration for a single minute out of 80. Often teams can sustain their effort for 50 or 60 minutes, maybe even 70 but it's highly unusual to do what we did and maintain the incredible intensity of our flat-out pressure for the whole 80 minutes.

ROBERTSON: *What was the big turning point of the match?*

SOLE: Actually, I think there were three, all in the second half. At the first scrum after half-time on the half-way line, England won their own put-in but instead of giving it to Rob Andrew, Mike Teague knocked-on trying to pick up at number eight. Andrew had a magnificent match for England and would almost certainly have planted a kick into our '22'. Instead we had a scrum on half-way, Gavin came into the line and Tony Stanger scored the winning try. Secondly, there was a priceless tackle by Scott Hastings on Rory Underwood to save a try and thirdly, our whole effort was epitomised when Will Carling looked dangerous in midfield near our line and not only was he tackled in the centre but almost our whole pack arrived instantly to thunder him backwards 20 yards. These three incidents showed our strength, determination and commitment both in attack and in defence.

ROBERTSON: *Who did you think were their potential match-winners?*

SOLE: The individuals most likely to win the game for England were Will Carling, Rory Underwood and Rob Andrew. As it turned out they all had only very limited opportunities but I thought Andrew had a superb game. He was the player who kept England in the match. His kicking was phenomenal.

ROBERTSON: *What did you say in your team talk in the changing room before the match?*

SOLE: I didn't say very much at all because I didn't need to. Ian McGeechan gave a highly emotional talk in the hotel before we left for the ground which had everyone close to tears and there was little more that needed saying. We knew we were the privileged 15 guys playing for Scots in every corner of the world. In the changing room I think I said something along the lines of 'No matter what happens in the next 80 minutes life will still go on but this afternoon we have a chance in a million to make history so let's go out and grab it with both hands.'

ROBERTSON: *Whose idea was it to walk out rather than run out on to the pitch before the match?*

SOLE: It was basically my idea, but I discussed it with the senior players, who were all in agreement. We wanted, I suppose, to show the crowd we were in control, disciplined, organized and ready for the biggest challenge of our lives. The response of the crowd was unforgettable. Their blood-curdling cheers lifted the whole team. Remember with the way tickets are distributed for home internationals there were 50,000 Scots in the crowd of 55,000. The team, *en bloc,* requested two verses, not one, of 'Flower of Scotland'. I sang the first verse but was so incredibly moved by the fantastic singing of the crowd I just couldn't get the words out for the second verse – I choked with emotion. The lyrics are highly charged and so was the occasion.

ROBERTSON: *Was this match the most enjoyable and satisfying game of rugby you have ever played?*

SOLE: Yes, it was, from every aspect – from the way we played, the atmosphere and the result.

INTERVIEW WITH GAVIN HASTINGS

ROBERTSON: *What made you confident that Scotland would be good enough to beat England after the three excellent English wins prior to Murrayfield?*

HASTINGS: I just felt we would approach the game in a different way and we would be capable of matching the English forwards which the other three countries had not been. England had also scored a few soft tries in the Championship where the tackling of the opposition had been pretty lax and there was no way they would score soft tries against us because our defensive organization and tackling has been a feature of our play throughout the last couple of seasons. We had beaten them at Murrayfield in similar circumstances in 1986 and in 1989 at Twickenham when they were hot favourites to beat us we had drawn 12–12 and shown them how difficult it was to score tries against us. In fact, apart from one penalty try, England had only scored two tries in their previous eight internationals against Scotland which means they crossed our line to score an average of once every four matches or every 320 minutes. So I'm the first to acknowledge they had played superbly all season especially against France and Wales, but I was also sure they would find the Scots a very different proposition and whatever other failings we might have it wouldn't be indecisive or weak tackling.

ROBERTSON: *How important was the fanatical support of the crowd?*

HASTINGS: Enormously important. It was an unbelievable, unique atmosphere which I've certainly never experienced previously. From the moment we walked on to the pitch, to the singing of 'Flower of Scotland', right up to the final whistle the support was out of this world. It was the noisiest international I've ever played in and it must have been very intimidating for the English players. This match was my 24th international for Scotland and I've only ever lost at Murrayfield once so there's no doubt playing at home is a huge advantage. Every time the whistle went there would be a momentary silence and then a tumultuous roar would follow if the referee signalled it was a Scottish put-in to the scrum or a Scottish penalty. Whenever the referee gave us anything, the noise was deafening and it was impossible not to be moved by it. The crowd inspired the whole team.

ROBERTSON: *Who were the key Scottish players?*

HASTINGS: I thought it was primarily a team effort but if I had to mention a few who were exceptionally influential I would choose Gary Armstrong for his tackling, his cover defence, his service and his spoiling of Richard Hill, Craig Chalmers for his control of the game, Finlay Calder and John Jeffrey for spearheading the forward effort in the open and also the mobility of the whole pack. However, in the final analysis our victory can be best summed up by the fact that every single one of our side hit top form on the day.

ROBERTSON: *Is it an over-simplification to say that just as Scotland were below par earlier in the Championship so England had an off-day at Murrayfield?*

HASTINGS: We certainly didn't hit top form until the Calcutta Cup game and there's no question that for England that was their only disappointing display in the Championship but I don't think it was

David Sole leads a charge in the Fijian match

Derek White scores against Ireland

Sean Lineen beats Philippe Sella to score against France

John Jeffrey on the rampage against France

It takes Camberabero, Sella, Mesnel and Lhermet to slow down Derek White

Finlay Calder and Gavin Hastings have support from **Damian Cronin** and Gary Armstrong

Chris Gray and Paul Burnell secure lineout ball against England

Jeremy Guscott scores England's try at Murrayfield – his third in four matches

Tony Stanger and Chris Gray celebrate Scotland's Grand Slam-winning try

Calder, Sole and Gray celebrate at the final whistle

Victorious captain David Sole is mobbed by the ecstatic crowd

David Sole presents his jersey to Master Peter Phillips after the Grand Slam match

Ian and Judy McGeechan with their kids Robert and Heather have plenty to smile about

Following a tradition set in 1984 The Royal Bank of Scotland commissioned a painting to commemorate the 1990 Grand Slam. Artist Ronnie Browne has a further link with Scottish rugby as a member of the Corries, the duo whose 'Flower of Scotland' was adopted this season as the team's official 'anthem'

because they all had an off-day, I think it was because we exerted so much pressure on them they simply weren't able to play the way they had in the other matches. Rob Andrew had an outstanding game but most of the other English players were unable to stamp their mark on the match in the way they had against France and Wales.

ROBERTSON: *What would you choose as the single most important moment of the game?*

HASTINGS: It would be easy to choose Tony Stanger's try which was crucial, but I would answer Craig Chalmers' kicking those early first-half penalties laid the basis of our victory. They lifted the team and the crowd. England, for their part, missed vital penalty kicks and they could argue that cost them victory.

ROBERTSON: *Was that the most enjoyable match of your career?*

HASTINGS: The two most rewarding and most enjoyable matches I've played in were the British Lions' victory in the Third Test in Sydney in 1989 and the Grand Slam game against England in 1990. Both are on a par but I could argue that the Lions victory was the more dramatic. We achieved that with just 15 players on our side; against England there were 50,015 people on our side – no contest.

The Grand Slam heroes before the English game

6. *Reflections*

Looking back over the four Grand Slam matches there were all sorts of highlights sprinkled liberally around, but I have no doubt when the dust settles my main abiding memory will be the England game. Funnily enough, it won't just be the game itself but it will be everything to do with that game – the two-week build-up, the day of the match, the match, the celebrations that evening and the various celebrations in the ensuing couple of weeks.

At no time in my previous 20 years in rugby can I remember being involved in such an exciting and emotional build-up. I found it electrifying and it must have been doubly so for the players. I was fortunate to have Jim Telfer in the coaching team because he had the distinct advantage of coaching the 1984 side to the Grand Slam. So it was handy to check with him in the fortnight from the end of the Wales game to the Calcutta Cup weekend that I did not forget anything of real importance.

There were a lot of memorable moments before, during and after the match, but there is no doubt the singing of 'Flower of Scotland' as the teams lined up was nothing short of thrilling. Until that moment I had never experienced an atmosphere like it. Hitherto, the singing of the crowd at Cardiff had come closest but this seemed to be even more forbidding and dramatic. The atmosphere was like the old days when there was that high terrace opposite the West Stand before the East Stand was built. And, in retrospect, if our special 'anthem' sent a shiver of excitement down my spine, it must have been very intimidating for the English. My school team, Fir Tree Middle School from Leeds, were at Murrayfield on the terraces and when I went into school on the following Monday Richard Halls, the master in charge in Edinburgh, who teaches P E and Craft, Design and Technology, recounted the chilling story of the big-match build-up.

For virtually all of them it was their first time at Murrayfield and they were thoroughly enjoying and soaking up the atmosphere when the band struck up the National Anthem. Richard told the boys, who were all in school uniform, to stand up straight and sing 'God Save the Queen' loudly and proudly, because they were representing England. He said it all sounded pretty good and he told the boys they'd done well, he was proud of them and they had certainly done their bit for the English team.

An ominous silence followed for a few moments while the Pipes and Drums of Queen Victoria School, Dunblane got themselves organized. Then the opening bars of 'Flower of Scotland' sounded and after the first couple of lines of the first verse, with a deafening volume able to be measured on the Richter scale, Richard said he suddenly felt he was the only Englishman in the whole ground. He had never before experienced such passion in a song and it seemed

Wade Dooley wins this lineout despite the close attention of Paul Burnell

to overpower and overwhelm the whole stadium. He said by the end of the second verse he was quite convinced he was Scottish himself.

Perhaps the most revealing statistic, as we look back at the last six years of Scottish rugby, is the fact that we have built two Grand Slam sides without a single player overlapping. That is most unusual especially when you consider that Jim and Finlay Calder are twins, between them they have won over fifty Scottish caps and yet they have never played in the same side and each went on a different British Lions tour – one in 1983 and the other in 1989.

After winning only one previous Grand Slam in 1925, it is a re-markable achievement to collect two more in 1984 and 1990, with two totally different teams. We had to rebuild in 1984 and again after the World Cup in 1987 but fortunately it is quite likely that the only player we are going to lose before the 1991 World Cup from the 1990 Grand Slam team is Finlay Calder. There is no reason why the rest of the squad should not be in contention for next year's Five Nations Championship and the World Cup in the autumn of 1991.

One of the great things about this side is that they have tremen-dous team spirit, and have evolved their own highly flexible style of play, which can only develop further and into a more sophisticated

David Sole means business as he walks on to the pitch followed by Kenny Milne before the Calcutta Cup match

form the more they practise and play together over the next year. I know it's possibly not unique for the same team to play in all four internationals unchanged in a season but it's nonetheless a worthwhile achievement and a tribute to the fitness of the squad.

As I reflect on the season I can't help emphasizing the importance of the very high quality we were fortunate in having in the really key positions – the spine of the team. The five players who make up the spine are the five most influential players in a side and they are the positions where it is extremely difficult to carry any passengers – hooker, number eight, scrum-half, fly-half, and full-back. Of course, there are important satellites around these stars who make a major contribution as well, but useful though good props undoubtedly are to the hooker and flankers are to the number eight and wing threequarters are to the full back in defence, the five key players comprise the spine of the side.

In Scotland's case the spine read Kenny Milne, Derek White, Gary Armstrong, Craig Chalmers and Gavin Hastings. I think it is significant that not one of the other sides in the Five Nations Championship could better our group. England came closest, with Brian

Craig Chalmers sells referee Fred Howard a dummy and unleashes his threequarters

Ian McGeechan in thoughtful mood as he masterminds Scotland's best ever season

Moore, Richard Hill and Rob Andrew all really outstanding players, and on at least a par with our trio. Mike Teague is a great forward, but flanker rather than number eight is probably his best position. When Dean Richards is in the side, with Teague on the flank, it is easy to understand how England are such a formidable side with four top-class players out of five in the spine of their team.

The fact that France had their most disappointing season for several years can be partly explained by the decline of the spine of their side. Ever since 1986 when they had Daniel Dubroca or Phillippe Dintrans at hooker, Laurent Rodriguez at number eight, Pierre Berbizier and Franc Mesnel at half-back and the incomparable Serge Blanco at full-back, it was no surprise when they finished at the top of the Championship four seasons in succession. But now they are not so strong at hooker, they have dropped Berbizier and Blanco is no longer quite the force he was. What is worse, they dropped Didier Camberabero from fly-half during the season and chopped and changed their five key players throughout the season.

Wales were able to match most countries at half-back where Robert Jones and David Evans enjoyed a good season in difficult circumstances, but in the other critical positions they found all too often the opposition had a better collection in the spine of their team than they had. Similarly, Ireland were particularly well served by Noel Mannion at number eight and Kenny Murphy at full-back and pretty well served by Brian Smith at fly-half; but as I said at the start of this analysis I would not have swapped my five players for any of the others in the Five Nations Championship.

On exactly the same basis I preferred the Lions spine last summer to the Wallabies one. There was nothing to choose between the half-backs – Rob Andrew and Robert Jones for the Lions and Nick Farr-Jones and Michael Lynagh for Australia – but I think we had the edge in the other positions, especially at full back, when you compare Gavin Hastings with Greg Martin. Similarly, I preferred hooker Brian Moore and number eight Dean Richards to Tom Lawton and Steve Tuynman.

The second most important group of players, after analysing the spine of a side, is the pivot five – the back row and the half-backs. This group includes, of course, three of the spine of the team, but the pivot five serve a special purpose as a link between the backs and forwards. They play a major role in attack as the front line of the creative playmakers and they are the backbone of the defence as the initial destroyers. Scotland have been very strong here in 1990, just as we were in 1984 for the last Grand Slam. Six years ago the pivot five were Jim Calder, Iain Paxton, and David Leslie, Roy Laidlaw and John Rutherford. In 1990 it read John Jeffrey, Derek White, and Finlay Calder, Gary Armstrong and Craig Chalmers.

There were several other factors which also contributed to our

The front row of Paul Burnell, Kenny Milne and David Sole prepare to join battle with the French

eventual success. I have mentioned already the fantastic team spirit and this made it easy for players and coaches to talk openly and freely at all our team meetings. This helped me enormously in deciding on the tactics for the next game because I knew what everyone involved in the squad was thinking. We were aware that we had not hit peak form in the first three internationals of the Championship even though we had a few very good passages in each of these games which included two away wins. After each of those games in Dublin, Edinburgh and Cardiff, when the team returned to the hotel around six or seven o'clock in the evening, there was a full team meeting to go over that afternoon's victory and to see where we needed to improve most for the next game. I stored all that information before formulating the plans for the following fortnight.

Interestingly enough, the fact that the players were self-critical after each of the games against Ireland, France, and Wales encouraged me because it showed that winning was no longer enough in itself – their level of expectation in the international arena was considerably higher than that. I like to think such a mixture of idealism and realism is something we've learned from the New Zealand All Blacks. They are never fully satisfied with just a win and it was good to find our players with the same positive, aggressive attitude.

Another important ingredient we developed during the season was patience. We talked about it from the Romanian match onwards and it applied to all four Championship games. It applied particularly to the two away matches which were very close, tight games and we knew we had to keep our concentration just as much when we were under pressure and having to play without the ball deep in defence as it was to grab those half-chances in attack when we did have possession. This is also part of the New Zealand ideology. If we did have the ball we made life very difficult for the opposition but we never panicked and we had so many layers of defence we were confident it would always be difficult for teams to score tries against us. We tried never to let the opposition seize the initiative, and, when we were in control, to make every chance and half-chance count.

One of the most fascinating aspects of this blanket defence which could become almost instantly transformed into a sweeping counter-attack was the remarkable mobility of the tight five forwards, coupled with their huge appetite for defence – their ruthless, abrasive tackling. It was often breathtaking to watch them sprint across the field and rattle in a priceless tackle to save a dangerous situation. They all performed these heroics, with David Sole and Kenny Milne just as devastating in setting up the next attack as in abruptly chopping down an opponent in defence.

In the final analysis I doubt any other tight-head prop put in more tackles in the Championship than Paul Burnell or any locks tackled harder or more often than Damian Cronin or Chris Gray. This mobility in attack and defence was a big bonus because we sacrificed nothing in our scrummaging. We held our own in the set-scrums at the very least in every match and certainly had an advantage over Ireland and Wales.

The lineout was a bit disappointing against Ireland but we worked very hard at that area of our game and it definitely improved and developed as the season progressed. With a fairly decent return from our set-piece play we were able to cash in on the efforts of the tight forwards with the superb play of our three loose forwards – John Jeffrey, Derek White and Finlay Calder, plus Derek Turnbull when he came on as a replacement in the Calcutta Cup game. Individually, they played brilliantly and collectively they were outstanding especially in the England match. They blend together just about perfectly; they have had a wonderful run over the past couple of years.

I reckon John Jeffrey had his best-ever season for Scotland because he's developed into the complete back-row player. He's always been good with the ball in his hands in attack, good at the lineout and a tremendous support player. Now he is good going back in defence and a bone-shuddering tackler, as Mark Jones the Welsh number eight discovered when John buried him over and over again at Cardiff. Derek White is another first-class footballer and with renewed confidence he has also had a great Championship. Finlay Calder played well in the early matches but saved his best for last when he was absolutely dynamic against England.

The half-backs, Gary Armstrong and Craig Chalmers, even though they struggled initially against Ireland, proved just how quickly they have matured and developed into established internationals. The Lions tour did them a power of good and they are now ready to take over the mantle from Roy Laidlaw and John Rutherford to guide Scotland's fortunes for the foreseeable future. Tactically sound in attack, they were like an extra pair of flankers in defence, ripping into tackles with real relish. They are both great competitors, they are real winners and they will fight every inch of the way to secure victory.

On that note, no one tackled better than the two centres, Scott Hastings and Sean Lineen. The thing I liked most about them is that they did it as a pair. They worked as a partnership in the centre and that made life very hard for their opponents. They were a revelation as a pairing, playing like twins, and they had tremendous pride in their performance which spread through the team. Both wings had their moments in attack and Tony Stanger scored some excellent tries in his first season in international rugby. He missed just one tackle in the Welsh game on Arthur Emyr when he was wrongfooted but he learned from that and he policed Rory Underwood successfully as he had done Patrice Lagisquet. He and Iwan Tukalo did everything that was asked of them and their defensive work, as well

The outstanding tackling of the Scottish forwards is exemplified here by David Sole upending Louis Armary

as the eight tries they scored between them in the six internationals, were crucial to our cause.

At full-back Gavin Hastings also had a very good year indeed. In fact, although Gavin only scored one try (against Fiji), I think he had his best season for Scotland as a full back. His tackling as always was utterly conclusive, his line kicking was outstanding and he was supremely confident under the high ball, as well as being fearless. Even if he did not join the line as often as usual as the extra man in attack, he was potentially dangerous and the opposition always had to check on him. When he did join the threequarter line he made a few sizeable dents.

It is also fair to say that having one of the world's great players there as the last line of defence and a constant threat in attack gives the whole team confidence. And if I had to pick a handful of special

Sean Lineen and Patrice Lagisquet chase the ball

highlights from the Grand Slam games I would certainly choose the start of the second half in the French match. We had the advantage of the wind in the first half and Blanco had great trouble punting into the wind. We only led 3–0 at half-time and we were anything but over-confident of victory. Blanco began the second half kicking the ball deep to Gavin. He caught it and belted it from near his own line right up to the half-way line into the slanting wind. Didier Cambera-bero's eyes nearly popped out of his head in disbelief and the whole crowd could feel the surge of confidence that gave the Scottish team. From that moment, we never looked back.

Gavin would have to feature again in my favourite highlights. He had a couple of shaky moments in the Irish game in the first half but when the chips were really down at the very end of the match, as we were clinging precariously to a three-point lead, Gavin magnificently caught a high, hanging, towering up-and-under from Brian Smith, stood on his feet as the whole Irish pack engulfed him and ensured we won the ball to allow Craig Chalmers to clear to touch and save the match. Gavin, now more than ever, has pride in the basic hard graft of full-back play, as well as still being dynamic in attack.

Then there was the incredible cover tackle by Craig Chalmers on the French wing Hontas when, with a despairing dive, he clipped his

Once again tenacious Scottish tackling halts Mike Teague's progress

heels and brought him down. Was that perhaps the best moment of the season? Or was it the phenomenal tackle by Scott Hastings on Rory Underwood towards the end of the English match when it looked as if the electrifying speed of Underwood would take him through the gap to score?

Or perhaps I should single out Gary Armstrong's priceless tackles on Richard Hill. Or the time Will Carling cut back inside menacingly near our line only to be stopped by a wall of navy blue jerseys and frogmarched 20 yards back towards his own line in double-quick time by half the Scottish side. Or Kenny Milne's deadly accurate throwing-in to the lineout against England as we kept swapping and switching the positions of our jumpers. Or perhaps John Jeffrey's series of try-saving tackles on Mark Jones at all those scrum

Will Carling, England's brilliant centre, is surrounded by Scottish players

fives on our line in Cardiff. Or perhaps the shared moments with the Princess Royal away from the spotlight after the internationals when she could talk about the fun and enjoyment she had had following our fortunes during the season. Or perhaps, or perhaps, or perhaps . . .

What I do know for sure is that I have a whole host of wonderful memories to look back on at the end of my most exciting season ever with Scotland. It's been a momentous time and it's been a fantastic thrill, privilege and pleasure to be involved with such a great bunch of guys. Perhaps the single most lasting memory will simply be the final whistle at the end of the English match as the ecstatic crowd swept across the pitch and the whole nation, from the Borders to John O'Groats, began the celebrations. Or perhaps the haunting strains of 'Flower of Scotland' before the match, or perhaps . . . or perhaps . . .

The agony for Brian Moore and the ecstasy for the Scottish fans as they cheer their heroes

7. The Players

DAVID SOLE

Club: Edinburgh Academicals. Caps: 25. Born: 8.5.62, Aylesbury. Height: 5′11″. Weight: 16st 6lbs.
International matches: 1986 F, W; 1987 I, F, W, E (World Cup), F, Z, R, NZ; 1988 I, F, W, E, A; 1989 W, E, I, F, Fj, R; 1990 I, F, W, E. Points: 4 – 1 try. British Lions to Australia 1989 1, 2, 3.

David Michael Barclay Sole has not missed an international match for his country since winning the first of his 25 caps against France in 1986. He was also an ever-present for the British Lions on their successful tour to Australia in 1989. His driving, athletic play and solid scrummaging has led to him being universally recognized as one of the leading players in the world. He was appointed captain of Scotland at the beginning of the 1989–90 season and was also honoured with the captaincy of the Barbarians against the 1989 All Blacks. He was educated at Blairmore School, Aberdeenshire, Glenalmond and Exeter University. He is a grain buyer for United Distillers Cereals Ltd.

GAVIN HASTINGS

Club: London Scottish. Caps: 24. Born: 3.1.62, Edinburgh. Height: 6′2″. Weight: 15st.
International matches: 1986 F, W, E, I, R; 1987 I, F, W, E (World Cup), F, Z, R, NZ; 1988 I, F, W, E, A; 1989 Fj, R; 1990 I, F, W, E. Points: 255 – 7T, 51P, 37C. British Lions – Australia 1,2,3. Points: BI 28 – 1T, 8P.

Andrew Gavin Hastings is within 18 points of emulating Andy Irvine's points record for Scotland. He would have almost certainly broken it this season but for an uncharacteristic loss of form which saw the goal-kicking duties pass to Craig Chalmers. In all other respects though Gavin Hastings was back to the form which saw him prominent as the backbone of the British Lions defence in Australia. As illustrated by his match-winning try, he also contributed a vital cutting edge in attack. He currently holds the Scottish points record for a championship season of 52 points. This year he has also successfully led London Scottish to the third division title. He is a quantity surveyor with Richard Ellis in London.

The front row of Paul Burnell, Kenny Milne and David Sole

TONY STANGER

Club: Hawick. Caps: 6. Born: 14.5.68, Hawick. Height: 6'2″. Weight: 13st 7lbs. International matches: 1989 Fj, R; 1990 I, F, W, E. Points: 24 – 6 tries.

Anthony George Stanger had a marvellous start to his international career, scoring two tries on his debut against Fiji in October 1989. That run of try-scoring form continued throughout the season, culminating in his match-winning and Grand Slam-winning try against England. He played his first game for Hawick whilst still a schoolboy at Hawick High School. He has also played for the club in the centre, the position in which he won five Scottish schools caps. He was educated at Wilton Primary School, Hawick High School and is a bank officer with The Royal Bank of Scotland.

SCOTT HASTINGS

Club: Watsonians. Caps: 23. Born: 4.12.64, Edinburgh. Height: 6'1″. Weight: 13st 6lbs. International matches: 1986 F, W, E, I, R; 1987 I, F, W (World Cup), R; 1988 I, F, W, A; 1989 W, E, I, F, Fj, R; 1990 I, F, W, E. Points: 16 – 4 tries. British Lions 1989 – Australia 2, 3.

Scott Hastings made history in the Second Test against Australia in 1989 when he and Gavin became the first brothers to play together for the Lions. Scott went on to play an outstanding role in the last two Tests and pulled off the tackle of the tour when playing on the wing against the Anzacs. Scott has been a virtual ever-present in the Edinburgh side since he made his debut in 1985. He spends the summer months trying to improve his golf handicap. He is an advertising account executive with Barkers in Edinburgh.

Tony Stanger also means business during his remarkable introduction to international rugby – six tries and six victories

SEAN LINEEN

Club: Boroughmuir. Caps: 10. Born: 25.12.61, Auckland, New Zealand. Height 6'1". Weight 13st 10lbs.
International matches: 1989 W, E, I, F, Fj, R; 1990 I, F, W, E.

Sean Raymond Patrick Lineen qualified to play for Scotland through his grandfather who came from the Hebrides. Sean's father, Terry, won 12 caps for the All Blacks as a five-eighth, a career which included all four tests against the 1959 British Lions. Sean has also played club rugby in Wales. He joined Boroughmuir in October 1988 and won his first cap just a few months later. His close understanding both in attack and defence with Scott Hastings has been one of the most impressive features of his play both for Scotland and Edinburgh. He is a property manager with Little-johns of Edinburgh.

IWAN TUKALO

Club: Selkirk. Caps: 22. Born: 5.3.61, Edinburgh. Height: 5'9". Weight: 12st 9lbs.
International matches: 1985 I; 1987 I, F, W, E (World Cup), F, Z, R, NZ; 1988 F, W, E, A; 1989 W, E, I, F, Fj; 1990 I, F, W, E. Points: 40 – 10 tries.

Iwan Tukalo has played in 21 of the last 23 cap internationals and has been a regular try-scorer. His 10 tries include a hat-trick in the record-breaking match against Ireland in 1989. He began his representative career as a scrum half for Scottish Schools in 1978. He has been on Scottish tours to Romania, North America, Spain and France and Japan. He was educated at Royal High in Edinburgh and is a senior engineer with British Gas.

Iwan Tukalo, who scored a try against France

CRAIG CHALMERS

Club: Melrose. Caps: 9. Born: 15.10.68, Galashiels. Height: 5'10". Weight: 12st 7lbs.
International matches: 1989 W, E, I, F, Fj; 1990 I, F, W, E. Points: 40 – 1T, 3C, 9P, 1DG. British Lions – Australia 1. Points: BI 6 – 1P, 1DG.

Craig Minto Chalmers stepped into the void left by the retirement of John Rutherford and immediately made his mark with a try and a drop goal on his debut against Wales. His first Championship season saw him firmly established and he was rewarded by selection for the British Lions party to tour Australia. He took over goal-kicking duties for Scotland in the 1989-90 season after a productive year for his club, Melrose. He was educated at Melrose Grammar School and Earlston and is a marketing representative with the South of Scotland Electricity Board.

GARY ARMSTRONG

Club: Jed-Forest. Caps: 11. Born: 30.9.66, Edinburgh. Height: 5'10". Weight: 13st.
International matches: 1988 A; 1989 W, E, I, F, Fj, R; 1990 I, F, W, E. Points: 4 – 1 try.

Gary Armstrong was one of the nine Scottish players on the British Lions tour to Australia in 1989. He ended the tour, in which he played in five of the 12 matches, as second-top try scorer with five tries. He settled into an immediate understanding with Craig Chalmers during the 1989 season which brought to mind, for many, the partnership of Roy Laidlaw and John Rutherford. Laidlaw has spent many hours with Gary Armstrong, both coming from the same club. He was educated at Jedburgh Grammar School and Dunfermline High School and works in Jedburgh.

*Gary Armstrong in full flow as he plays his best game for Scotland in the
Grand Slam decider*

KENNY MILNE

Club: Heriot's Former Pupils. Caps: 10. Born: 1.12.61, Edinburgh. Height: 6′. Weight: 14st 4lbs. International matches: 1989 W, E, I, F, Fj, R; 1990 I, F, W, E. Points: 4 – 1 try.

Kenneth Stuart Milne created history on winning his first cap against Wales in 1989. Alongside him was elder brother Iain, the first time two brothers have played in the front row for Scotland. Kenny is part of a famous rugby-playing family with other brother David having played for Scotland B. Together they make for a formidable front row. His accurate throwing to the lineout was a feature of Scotland's play this season. He was educated at George Heriot's School and Stevenson College. He is a sales representative with Barr Printers, Leith.

PAUL BURNELL

Club: London Scottish. Caps: 9. Born: 29.9.65, Edinburgh. Height: 6′. Weight: 16st 3lbs. International matches: 1989 E, I, F, Fj, R; 1990 I, F, W, E.

Andrew Paul Burnell is very much one of the unsung heroes of the Scottish side. His sturdy scrummaging and whole-hearted commitment never faltered during the international season. He has played all his senior rugby in England, for Marlow, Harlequins and Leicester before joining London Scottish. He might have played against Scotland in the final match for whilst with Leicester he played for the Midlands in the Divisional Championship. He has been a regular for the Anglo-Scots since 1987. He was educated at Blue Coat School, Reading and Leicester Polytechnic. He is a sales representative for Lease and Finance Services in Reading.

CHRIS GRAY

Club: Nottingham. Caps: 10. Born: 11.7.60, Haddington. Height: 6'5". Weight 16st 12lbs.
International matches: 1989 W, E, I, F, Fj, R; 1990 I, F, W, E. Points: 4 – 1 try.

Christopher Anthony Gray has had a busy year, playing in all Scotland's games as well as captaining his club, Nottingham, who enjoyed a late run of success in the Courage League, beating the respective favourites for the title, Bath and Gloucester. He first played for Edinburgh Academicals at the age of 18. He has toured both Zimbabwe and Japan with Scotland and made four appearances for Scotland B. He was educated at Gordonstoun, Edinburgh Academy and Edinburgh University. He is a dental surgeon in Nottingham.

DAMIAN CRONIN

Club: Bath. Caps: 15. Born: 17.4.63, West Germany. Height: 6'6". Weight: 16st 10lbs.
International matches: 1988 I, F, W, E, A; 1989 W, E, I, F, Fj, R; 1990 I, F, W, E. Points: 8 – 2 tries.

Damian Francis Cronin has been an ever-present in the Scottish second row since making his debut against Ireland in 1988. His rugged play in the loose and combativeness in the lineout have been a feature of the Scottish pack. He has also established himself as first-choice lock at Bath this season. He has toured both Zimbabwe and Japan with Scotland and represented the Home Unions XV which beat France in Paris in October 1989. He was educated at Campion School, Essex and Prior Park College, Bath. He is a sales manager in Cardiff.

Chris Gray played a key role at the lineout for Scotland, especially in the final three matches

JOHN JEFFREY

Club: Kelso. Caps: 28. Born: 25.3.59, Kelso. Height: 6'4″. Weight: 14st 7lbs.
International matches: 1984 A; 1985 I, E; 1986 F, W, E, I, R; 1987 I, F, W, E (World Cup), F, Z, R; 1988 I, W, A; 1989 W, E, I, F, Fj, R; 1990 I, F, W, E. Points: 36 – 9 tries.

John Jeffrey has been one of the outstanding members of the Scottish side over the last six years. He has scored a record number of international tries for a Scottish forward – nine in all. He was in the British Lions party which toured Australia in 1989 but failed to win a test place. Despite starting on the junior side in the Scottish Trial, John Jeffrey came through to have perhaps his finest ever season. In 1988–89 he proved an inspirational captain of Kelso who collected the Division One Championship. After reading agricultural economics at Newcastle University, Jeffrey returned to his home town of Kelso where he assists with the management of the family farm.

DEREK TURNBULL

Club: Hawick. Caps: 4. Born: 2.10.61, Hawick. Height: 6'4″. Weight: 15st 7lbs.
International matches: 1987 (World Cup) NZ; 1988 F, E; 1990 E (R).

Derek James Turnbull was the only change in the Scottish side during the Championship season, coming on as a replacement for Derek White during the final match against England. He is very similar to White in that he has played representative rugby in every back-five position of the scrum. He has represented Scotland at several levels as well as several positions and has been an invaluable member of the 1990 Championship squad. He was educated at Hawick High School.

DEREK WHITE

Club: London Scottish. Caps: 24. Born: 30.1.58, Dunbar. Height: 6′4″. Weight: 15st 12lbs.
International matches: 1982 F, W, A (1, 2); 1987 W, E (World Cup), F, R, NZ; 1988 I, F, W, E, A; 1989 W, E, I, F, Fj, R; 1990 I, F, W, E. Points: 24 – 6 tries. British Lions 1989 – A (1).

Derek Bolton White has played his international rugby in various positions – flanker, lock and number eight. He has won seven caps as a lock, three as a flanker, two as a flanker who was switched during the match to number eight and 12 caps as a number eight. The latter position is his preferred one which he filled for the British Lions in Australia in 1989 during which he played in the First Test. That trip saw his confidence rise having established himself as a genuine international number eight. That showed in his first game in the Five Nations this season when he scored twice against Ireland. He has recently moved south of the border and is a sales manager with Mercia Diagnostics Ltd in Guildford.

FINLAY CALDER

Club: Stewart's Melville FP. Caps: 26. Born: 20.8.57, Haddington. Height: 6′2″. Weight: 15st 7lbs.
International matches: 1986 F, W, E, I, R; 1987 I, F, W, E (World Cup), F, Z, R, NZ; 1988 I, F, W, E; 1989 W, E, I, F, R; 1990 I, F, W, E. Points: 8 – 2 tries. British Lions: 1989 – A (1, 2, 3).

Finlay Calder had a very competitive childhood with three rugby-playing brothers in the family. Finlay followed twin brother Jim into the Scottish side as flanker, displacing him in 1986. The twins were joined by brother John on the 1982 Scottish tour to Australia when he flew out as a replacement. Twin brother Jim also played in a Grand Slam side in 1984 and in fact scored the clinching try against France at Murrayfield. Finlay led Scotland in the 1989 Championship season and was then honoured with the captaincy of the successful Lions party which toured Australia. Finlay is a grain shipper with Ceres (UK) in Leith.

Appendix

IRELAND 10 SCOTLAND 13

Teams:
IRELAND – K. Murphy (Constitution); M. Kiernan (Dolphin), B. Mullin (Blackrock College), D. Irwin (Instonians), K. Crossan (Instonians); B. Smith (Oxford University), F. Aherne (Lansdowne); J. Fitzgerald (Young Munster), J. McDonald (Malone), D. Fitzgerald (Lansdowne); P. O'Hara (Sunday's Well) (rep. P. Collins, London Irish), D. Lenihan (Constitution), W. Anderson (Dungannon) (capt.), P. Matthews (Wanderers), N. Mannion (Corinthians).

SCOTLAND – G. Hastings (London Scottish); A. Stanger (Hawick), S. Hastings (Watsonians), S. Lineen (Boroughmuir), I. Tukalo (Selkirk); C. Chalmers (Melrose), G. Armstrong (Jed-Forest); D. Sole (Edinburgh Academicals) (capt.), K. Milne (Heriot's FP), P. Burnell (London Scottish), J. Jeffrey (Kelso), C. Gray (Nottingham), D. Cronin (Bath), F. Calder (Stewart's Melville FP), D. White (London Scottish).
Referee: C. Norling (WRU).

Scorers:
IRELAND: Try: J. Fitzgerald. Penalty Goals: M. Keirnan (2).
SCOTLAND: Tries: D. White (2). Conversion: C. Chalmers. Penalty goal: C. Chalmers.

SCOTLAND 21 FRANCE 0

Teams:
SCOTLAND – G. Hastings (London Scottish); A. Stanger (Hawick), S. Hastings (Watsonians), S. Lineen (Boroughmuir), I. Tukalo (Selkirk); C. Chalmers (Melrose), G. Armstrong (Jed-Forest); D. Sole (Edinburgh Academicals) (capt.), K. Milne (Heriot's FP), P. Burnell (London Scottish), J. Jeffrey (Kelso), C. Gray (Nottingham), D. Cronin (Bath), F. Calder (Stewart's Melville FP), D. White (London Scottish).

FRANCE – S. Blanco (Biarritz); P. Hontas (Biarritz), P. Sella (Agen), F. Mesnel (Racing Club), P. Lagisquet (Bayonne); D. Camberabero (Béziers), H. Sanz (Narbonne); M. Pujolle (Nice), L. Armary (Lourdes), P. Ondarts (Biarritz), J-M. Lhermet (Montferrand), T. Devergie (Nîmes), O. Roumat (Dax), A. Carminati (Béziers), L. Rodriguez (Dax) (capt.).
Referee: Fred Howard (RFU).

Scorers:
SCOTLAND: Tries: Calder, Tukalo. Conversions: Chalmers (2). Penalty goals: G. Hastings, Chalmers (2).

WALES 9 SCOTLAND 13

Teams:

WALES – P. Thorburn (Neath); M. Hall (Cardiff), M. Ring (Cardiff), A. Bateman (Neath), A. Emyr (Swansea); D. Evans (Cardiff) (rep. A. Clement, Swansea, R. Jones (Swansea) (capt.); B. Williams (Neath), K. Phillips (Neath), J. Pugh (Neath), M. Perego (Llanelli), P. Davies (Llanelli), G. Llewellyn (Neath), R. Collins (Cardiff), M. Jones (Neath).

SCOTLAND – G. Hastings (London Scottish); A. Stanger (Hawick), S. Hastings (Watsonians), S. Lineen (Boroughmuir), I. Tukalo (Selkirk); C. Chalmers (Melrose), G. Armstrong (Jed-Forest); D. Sole (Edinburgh Academicals) (capt.), K. Milne (Heriot's FP), P. Burnell (London Scottish), J. Jeffrey (Kelso), C. Gray (Nottingham), D. Cronin (Bath), F. Calder (Stewart's Melville FP), D. White (London Scottish).
Referee: R. Hourquet (France).

Scorers:
WALES: Try: Emyr. Conversion: Thorburn. Penalty Goal: Thorburn.
SCOTLAND: Try: Cronin. Penalty Goals: Chalmers (3).

SCOTLAND 13 ENGLAND 7

Teams:
SCOTLAND – G. Hastings (London Scottish); A. Stanger (Hawick), S. Hastings (Watsonians), S. Lineen (Boroughmuir), I. Tukalo (Selkirk); C. Chalmers (Melrose), G. Armstrong (Jed-Forest); D. Sole (Edinburgh Academicals) (capt.), K. Milne (Heriot's FP), P. Burnell (London Scottish), J. Jeffrey (Kelso), C. Gray (Nottingham), D. Cronin (Bath), F. Calder (Stewart's Melville FP), D. White (London Scottish) (rep. D. Turnbull, Hawick).

ENGLAND – S. Hodgkinson (Nottingham); S. Halliday (Bath), J. Guscott (Bath), W. Carling (Harlequins) (capt.), R. Underwood (Leicester); R. Andrew (Wasps), R. Hill (Bath); P. Rendall (Wasps), B. Moore (Nottingham), J. Probyn (Wasps), M. Skinner (Harlequins), P. Ackford (Harlequins), W. Dooley (Preston Grasshoppers), P. Winterbottom (Harlequins), M. Teague (Gloucester).
Referee: David Bishop (NZ).

Scorers:
SCOTLAND: Try: Stanger. Penalties: Chalmers (3).
ENGLAND: Try: Guscott. Penalty: Hodgkinson.